One, Two, Three...

Also by Eleanor Craig:
P.S. YOUR NOT LISTENING

One, Two, Three... The Story of Matt, a Feral Child

Eleanor Craig

McGraw-Hill Book Company
New York   St. Louis   San Francisco
Düsseldorf   Mexico   Toronto

Book design by Milton Jackson.
Copyright © 1978 by Eleanor Craig.
All rights reserved.
Printed in the United States of America.
No part of this publication may be reproduced,
stored in a retrieval system, or transmitted
in any form or by any means, electronic, mechanical,
photocopying, recording, or otherwise, without the
prior written permission of the publisher.

1234567890BPBP78321098

Library of Congress Cataloging in Publication Data

Craig, Eleanor.
One, two, three . . .: the story of Matt, a feral
child.
1. Feral children—Cases, clinical reports,
statistics. I. Title.
RJ507.F47C7   618.9′28′9   78-6683
ISBN 0-07-013342-5

The case history of the "feral child" herein is a composite of a number of cases of the problems faced by the social service and medical profession in the diagnosis, treatment, and development of capabilities of such children. All names, dates, and locations affecting such cases have been changed to protect the innocent.

For Ann, Richard, Bill, and Ellen

With appreciation to:

Don Congdon,
Ann Craig,
Virginia Gough,
Paul Green,
Barry Kasdan,
Nancy Kelly,
Bruce Lee,
Lotte Perutz,
Shirley Sarkin,
Leon Tec, M.D.,
and
Edith Vogel.

Chapter 1

I T was five-fifteen when the phone down at the reception desk began to ring with annoying persistence. Everyone else had gone home, and I had stayed behind to dictate two reports in what I had hoped would be peace and quiet. After about the twentieth ring, I decided that I'd have to answer: "Harrison County Counselling Center, Eleanor Craig speaking."

"Yes ma'am." The caller cleared his throat. "Frank Barringer here. I understand you help kids who ain't exactly right. Now, my son has problems and I wanta get him straightened out. Is that the kinda work you do?"

"It depends on your son's problems, Mr.

Barringer." I wrote down his name on a message pad. "We'd need more information before we'd know if we could help your son. We have to meet with the parents as well as the child."

"Lissen, Miss," he bristled. "What I'm trying to tell you is my son can't go nowhere till someone comes to the house and teaches him how to mind. Now I told my wife that I'm askin' for a worker here tomorrow—319 Burley Street." Suddenly his authoritative tone changed to a husky, pleading whisper.

"Please come. We fight about Matt all the time."

The next day, lunch was my only free hour.

Leora, my supervisor, was skeptical. "Sure, go if you're willing," she said. "If we aren't the right agency, maybe you can direct them elsewhere."

The homes on Burley Street had been built twenty years earlier as rental housing for low-income families. Time had not been kind to the structures. Poorly maintained, many now were vacant, with weeds growing around them as high as the windowsills. Number three-nineteen was the last gray house on the right, the only one on the street surrounded by a high fence.

A German shepherd raced toward me as I got out of the car. Fortunately the gate was shut and locked. Each time I shouted "Hello!" the dog charged at the metal fence, barking sharply; but no one inside the house acknowledged the commotion. Frustrated, I rattled the gate and the dog went into a frenzy. There was nothing more I could do, so I walked slowly back to the car and got in. As I drove away, I was sure that I spotted someone peeking out from behind a curtain in the front window.

The following morning, as I was telling Leora of my bizarre experience, Mr. Barringer called again. "Look, Miss, I'm sorry." He sounded genuinely upset. "My wife promised that if you come back today, she'll let you in."

By now I was really curious and, back on Burley Street at noon, I could see that someone had prepared for my visit. The snarling dog was securely chained; the gate to the yard was open. As I walked up to the front door, I could hear what I thought was a baby's crying—the voice so frail, the intake of breath so rapid, that I expected to find a newborn child somewhere inside the house.

I knocked. No one answered. The crying didn't stop. I rapped harder, then harder again, when someone finally opened the door slightly. I could see that it was dark inside, the curtains drawn, and I could barely distinguish the outline of the woman whose form blended into shadows. What stunned me was the sight of the large, naked boy she was carrying in her arms, his bare skin illuminated by a shaft of light from the door that cast an eerie glow on his body. He appeared to be as big as an eight-year-old, but the sounds he was making were those of an infant. It had been his crying that I had heard earlier.

Shocked, I didn't know what to say. The woman of the house must have seen the astonishment in my eyes.

"I can't talk today," she blurted. "My son's too upset."

She slammed the door in my face.

Back at the center, I decided that if Mr. Barringer should call again, I'd insist, demand even, that he bring his family in for consultation. I'd already spoken with one of our psychiatric consultants, Dr. Diamond, who agreed to do a psychiatric evaluation of the mysterious child. If the family refused to come in, based on what I had reported, Dr. Diamond suggested that we refer the case to an agency that was geared to making home visits.

I hoped that this wouldn't be necessary, but, backed up by Dr. Diamond's authority, I was able to speak more forcefully than usual when Mr. Barringer called again. "Bring in your wife and son this Thursday morning at ten," I told him. "Dr. Diamond will see all of you together. He will try to help you with your son."

I was sure the Barringers wouldn't show up. But on Thursday morning, I found myself looking out the window time and again when, at a little past ten, a battered, yellow panel truck, its sides carrying advertising for a local laundry, pulled slowly into the parking lot. The driver, a middle-aged white man wearing a dark green uniform, jumped out and walked quickly to the passenger side. At first, he stood gesturing beside the door. He seemed to be pleading. Then angrily, he opened the door, reached into the truck and dragged out a writhing, screaming boy, who kicked and beat at him with his fists.

A small, plump woman slipped out of the truck. The boy stopped pummeling the man and leapt at her from the front, locking his legs around her hips and his arms around her neck, the force of his leap making her take several steps backwards. Yet she began patting him on the back as if she were holding an infant. Slowly, the trio moved toward the Center.

Both secretaries in the front office stared as the man held the door open for the odd pair. People in the waiting room strained to get a glimpse of what was going on, perhaps expecting from the infant-like sounds to see a sick baby. Instead, upon seeing the tiny, fair-skinned woman holding a huge boy, patients exchanged puzzled glances and shrugs, and began whispering to each other.

The boy, whose naked body I had glimpsed on my visit to Burley Street, was now bundled in a navy-blue parka with the hood tied tightly under his chin. Silky wisps of apricot-colored hair fell onto his forehead. His eyes were hollow—totally blank—like tiny portholes surrounded by deep purple circles. His nose and mouth were pressed deep into the hollow of the woman's shoulder, muffling his interminable crying.

The mother's hair was a shade darker than her son's; it hung long and thick, almost reaching her waist. From the back, the straight hair gave her the appearance of a teen-ager. But her face was tired and worn. Etched across her forehead were three long parallel wrinkles; deep furrows ran from the sides of both nostrils to the edges of her mouth. And without makeup, her coloring was so fair that the lines on her face were more prominent than her eyebrows or lips. Her jaw was set in a pugnacious look, but it was belied by her frightened eyes that never left her husband's face.

From a distance, Frank Barringer's slick-backed hair made him look younger than when he came closer. His eyes were dark and black, angry eyes, I thought to myself; and his cheeks were scarred and weatherbeaten. His nose had the wide, bumpy bridge of an unlucky boxer. He approached me with a jaunty swagger and shook hands with a painful firmness. He was, I suspected, trying to show me that being in the Center did not intimidate him.

I took the three of them to the doctor's office, then found myself pacing the hall as their interview progressed. Within a few minutes, Dr. Diamond was ushering Mrs. Barringer and her son, who was shrieking at the top of his lungs, toward the front door.

"Why don't you two wait in the car," said Dr. Diamond, almost yelling so that his voice would carry over the child's high-pitched screaming. "I want to talk with your husband a little longer."

As the mother carried the boy down the steps, Dr. Diamond stood staring at the two of them. He was, I had thought, truly unshakable. Now he was visibly upset. Hair rumpled, his shirt tail hanging out, tie askew, he was shaking his head in despair when he caught my eye. Without saying anything, he charged back to his office.

Going back to my desk, I found it impossible to work. About fifteen minutes later, Dick Diamond appeared in my doorway, mopping his brow with a handkerchief.

"God, what an ordeal!" He slumped into the chair next to my desk. Rolling his head back, he took several deep breaths before he spoke again. "You won't believe it." He was taking a small notebook from his breast pocket and he started to read from one of the pages.

"The boy's name is Matt. He was born on December ninth, so he's six years and three months of age. He cannot talk. He never has."

Oh Lord, I thought to myself, the prognosis is worse than I thought it would be. If a child hasn't spoken by the age of five, the chances are he never will.

". . . motor development," Dr. Diamond

was saying. "The boy runs around the house, but you can't prove it by me. His mother wouldn't put him down. He's impossible to manage. He has violent tantrums. He's unpredictable. The parents have spanked him, even locked him in his room, but it only makes him worse.

"The mother still feeds the child. He isn't toilet trained. He goes to sleep every night in a corner of the kitchen on the floor. His parents carry him to bed when he's asleep. And listen to this," Dr. Diamond was winding up his summary. "The boy tyrannizes the parents with obsessive rituals. He takes bottles—anything that comes in a glass container like shaving lotion or salad dressing—and pours the contents down the toilet. He then lines up the empty bottles on his windowsill and won't let the parents touch them. If they do touch them, he attacks them. From this interview I would conclude that the boy is too retarded to qualify for treatment here."

"Who would handle this case?" I asked. "I can't think of any agency who would take it on."

Dr. Diamond looked at me sharply. "Oh—do you want to become involved?"

"I'm terrified by the idea, if you really want to know. But there's something there, maybe it's the look in the boy's eyes. I just can't believe there isn't something locked up inside him. It doesn't feel right. That's the only way I can express it."

"Do you realize what you'd be getting into?" Dr. Diamond asked. "Do you know how much time you'd have to spend with the mother just to get to the point where she'd let you help her son?"

"Maybe that's it," I said. "It's not just the boy alone. I really wonder what's going on with those parents that they've waited so long to look for help."

"Okay." He shrugged, tucking the notebook back into his jacket pocket. "Why don't you try working with the family for six weeks? By that time your clinical observations should be ready for presentation to the staff for formal evaluation."

Six weeks. I wondered if it would give me enough time.

Before I could voice the question, Dr. Diamond was leaving. He paused, his hand on the doorknob.

"I don't envy you the task you are about to undertake," he said slowly. "This boy is as wild as if he'd been raised by animals. In fact I would have to describe him as a feral child."

Chapter 2

AFTER my conversation with Dr. Diamond, I worked with three troubled young boys and a pregnant teen-ager during the afternoon. My evening was spent in a meeting with several men who were discussing the growing problems of raising children in single-parent homes.

It was a tiring day, not unlike the others I'd experienced since I'd joined the counselling center three years ago. But, unlike the other social workers on the staff, my background had been in special education. And, for four years before joining the Center, I'd taught children with emotional problems.

I loved my teaching job. But eventually I'd

felt that it was draining me—that I needed time for self-renewal. So I had taken a year's leave of absence to commute to a local college for a master's degree in counselling while my husband, Bill, was in Europe doing research on his book.

My four children were delighted that I, too, had homework for a year. In turn, I enjoyed going with them, one at a time, to do research at the library. At the year's end I had planned to return to teaching, but Leora Kurtz, chief social worker at the Harrison County Counselling Center, called to offer me a job.

The hours proved to be longer than in my previous job; in fact, the clinic stayed open two evenings a week. There were times when not being available to my children was extremely difficult.

I had given up trying to keep the house pristine, the meals like clockwork. I'd stopped pretending I didn't lead a double life. But it took a family conference to settle the matter. "We'd be glad to help you more," the children told me, "if you'd try not to act like you're the one who's got to do it all . . ."

Mine was a challenging job, with a chance to continue to learn. I knew it was right for me. I hoped it would prove right for the members of my family, too.

"I'll be fired if I try to drive to the Center every week," Mr. Barringer pleaded when I called.

Transporting Mrs. Barringer and Matt was

becoming a major problem. They were too difficult to ask a volunteer driver to handle. Finally I thought of Ceil Black, a friend with whom I'd worked in special education. By chance, she had become a social worker at the school nearest the Barringers. "You'll want to get to know them," I cajoled. "Someday you'll be looking for a program for the boy."

Ceil groaned at my description of the boy's behavior but agreed to drive them for the diagnostic sessions. School social workers are involved in implementing the state law that mandates towns to either provide education for those children who have special needs, or to pay for their training elsewhere.

But Mr. Barringer called on Wednesday morning, a few minutes before they were due to arrive. "The kid wouldn't let my wife put his clothes on today. I told her," he sighed, "she's gotta start earlier next week."

Seven days later, I stood at the window looking down on Ceil's green Ford as it veered into the parking lot. Nothing happened when she opened the rear door. Then Mrs. Barringer's feet slid hesitantly from the car to the pavement. Slowly, she lifted the crying child from the car and held him as if they were one. She carried him grimly along the sidewalk to the door of the clinic. Watching her, I felt like leaning out the window to cheer her progress. Instead, I just hurried down the stairs to open the door for them.

She answered my "good morning" with a fleeting grimace, while her son began to howl even louder. I wondered whether he was responding to my voice or reacting to the fear and tension in his mother's body. I decided to say nothing more on the way upstairs; but Marsha, the receptionist, looked up with a cheery greeting. The child's screams became excruciating. I kept walking toward the staircase, fighting the impulse to cover my ears.

Suddenly, I realized that Mrs. Barringer's footsteps no longer echoed mine. Looking around, I saw that she'd begun inching backward, away from me. I made brief contact with her panic-stricken eyes before she suddenly turned away and rushed out the door.

I called out, but she kept running along the walk toward Ceil's car, the boy screeching and jouncing in her arms. I caught Ceil's startled expression as she looked up from her book. As they got in, Ceil shrugged helplessly in my direction and then drove away. I was keenly disappointed. Mrs. Barringer had at least gone into Dr. Diamond's office on her first visit to the Center. Why was she more frightened, today, with me?

The next week I was making coffee in the tiny kitchen, wondering whether Mrs. Barringer would keep her appointment, when Marsha called in that Ceil's car had arrived. Afraid of frightening her, I watched from inside while Mrs. Barringer carried the screaming child from the parking lot up the sidewalk. I held open the door but neither of us spoke.

This time I walked behind her to prevent her from changing her mind, as she had before. She paused for a moment by the door of the waiting room to readjust her grip on her son, but she seemed unaware that people inside were staring and whispering. Finally, panting heavily, she carried her son up the fifteen stairs, then stopped at the door of my office.

"It's okay," I said, trying to fathom why she was hesitating. "Most people feel afraid at first."

She craned her neck to peer into the room, then tentatively stepped over the threshold, toward the chair to the left of my desk. Her breathing was labored as she eased herself and the child down onto the cushioned seat. The boy, whimpering now, landed as she'd carried him, his legs straddling her lap, his back to me.

Her eyes darted wildly around the room, surveying all its contents. My office was small, but I liked its coziness. The walls were white and I'd painted the child-sized table and chair royal blue to match the floor-length curtains. There were pots of philodendron on both windowsills, and three colorful lithographs on the wall.

A blackboard and a dart target were nailed to the closet door. All the other play materials were purposely kept from sight, on the shelves in the closet. I watched Matt burrowing against his mother's body and wondered whether he would ever leave her lap to find those toys, whether he would ever begin to reveal through play the fears and fantasies, the wishes and anxieties that might account for his terror.

I thought of others who'd been here before him: a child in foster-care who repeatedly used the puppets to play out scenes of a mother sending her baby away, because the baby was "bad," and the boy who darted around the room with a plastic gun in each hand acting out episodes of terrifying violence. Some children coveted every item, satisfied with none, littering the floor with blocks, dolls, cars and soldiers. Others never ventured to the closet but spent their time pacing around the perimeter of the room, or huddling under the little table.

Once again, I looked at the pair to my left. I was struck by how alike they looked—with their reddish hair and light blue eyes. Yet as I drew my chair closer to them, I had a mental image of two frightened monkeys in a zoo. This mother and child were locked together with no hint of affection— using each other's bodies as shields, barriers between themselves and me. The boy kept up his relentless crying. I wondered how she could stand this constant irritant. My own head was beginning to pound.

"Does he cry like this at home?" I asked, suddenly realizing that I'd never heard her talk.

She didn't reply but dug into her white plastic shoulder bag, drew out a baby bottle filled with milk and placed it in his hands. He threw back his head, sucking noisily on the nipple.

I repeated the question, postponing any comment on the bottle. Yet the sight of her offering it to him discouraged me. It epitomized the irony of my wish to be optimistic about this case. And whose need was the bottle fulfilling? Did it indicate the only level on which this six-year-old child could function? Or was it the level at which she wanted to keep him?

While he drank, she began tugging at the waist of his beige sweater, trying to pull it off over his head. It was too small and she was having a difficult time. I wondered why both wore such ill-fitting clothes. When she finally had the sweater raised to the point where she had to take his bottle momentarily, he began making deep, throaty, growling noises, like a dog defending a bone.

Her hands were trembling as she pulled the sweater back down and began smoothing it out on his body. But he kept up the growling noises and once his arms were free he began to pound his fists against her face and breasts.

"Don't hurt me!" she cried. She spread her fingers to protect her eyes. It was the first thing I'd ever heard her say. He punched her cheeks and hands—faster, harder.

"No-no," she sobbed.

I watched, appalled. I'd seen other children attack their mothers, but never with such animalistic ferocity. Would he attack me, too, if I tried to interfere? I decided to wait a moment longer, hoping she herself could make him stop.

"Please!" she cried in a husky voice. "Please don't hurt me!"

Just as I leaned forward to grab his arms, he slumped against her chest, picked the bottle up from her lap, raised it to his lips. Closing his eyes, he drank.

His mother's face was swollen with scarlet bruises; her nose was running as tears poured down her cheeks. I handed her the Kleenex and we sat without speaking while she wiped her eyes. I was grateful for the silence, for the chance to gather my thoughts, and stunned by what I'd witnessed.

"Has he—" I found it difficult to speak. "Has he hit you like that before?" Avoiding my eyes, she began to rock her son in her arms.

"Matt mustn't be allowed to hurt you, Mrs. Barringer," I said. "It's harmful for both of you if you let him do that." Suddenly she started to sob. Her shudders shook the child, who sucked more furiously on the rubber nipple.

"He hits you a lot?" I asked when she was calmer. Sniffling, she drew out another tissue. I knew the unspoken answer.

I pulled my chair closer to hers. "Next time it happens," I said, "grab each of his wrists tightly and tell him firmly he's not allowed to hurt you. Don't let go till you're sure he'll stop. Do you think you can do that?"

She blew her nose.

"Will you try that, Mrs. Barringer?"

She shrugged noncommittally.

Suddenly I was completely exasperated. If she weren't willing to stop her son's attacks, there was no point in our continuing to meet. It became terribly important to get a sense of her commitment. "What is it you hope to accomplish coming here with Matt?" I realized my voice sounded hard.

"Frankie," she murmured, still wiping her nose. "Frankie wants him to mind."

The boy began sucking air through the bottle. Enraged that it was empty now, he held it by the nipple and banged it against the back of the chair.

"So that's what your *husband* wants," I persisted above Matt's mounting shrieks. "He wants your son to mind. Now, what about *you*? Is that what you want, too?"

She shrugged and again began to rock the boy, who gradually grew calmer, his cries gentled to a whimper. Tears coursed down her face, faster than she was able to wipe them away. I sat watching her, listening for some response. I hoped in her silence she was reflecting on the reasons for her sadness. I chose not to offer any comfort. Perhaps when she felt she'd suffered enough, she'd make a decision to change.

Slowly the clock ticked out the rest of the hour.

I intended to meet them downstairs the

following week, but the intercom buzzed while I sat at my desk.

"I couldn't stop her." Marsha sounded apologetic. "They're on their way up."

"That's okay . . ." I was both glad and surprised that Mrs. Barringer would come upstairs on her own, but suddenly the door was kicked open so forcefully that plaster chips flaked from the wall where the doorknob banged against it.

She stood framed in the doorway, holding the wailing boy. "I know!" she yelled harshly. He began to scream. "I know what youse stinkin' people do. An' I'm tellin' you you're never gonna get my son!" Her cheeks were flushed, her face contorted. "That's all I came t' tell ya. We ain't never comin' back!"

She turned around abruptly, heading toward the stairs. Matt stared back over her shoulder, eyes wide and dry, mouth ajar, screeching shrilly.

"No one here would try to take Matt away," I hurried after them. "We don't . . ."

"Ha!" she sneered. "I bin in places like this before." She started down the first step, one hand gripping the bannister, the other around her son. "An' I'm just warnin' you . . ."

Doors left and right along the long hallway began to creak open. Faces cautiously peered out at us, one or two from each office. Leora's gray head appeared suddenly. She was frowning at the interruption.

Ignoring the audience, I tried desperately to

stop Mrs. Barringer, hoping this crisis would prove a breakthrough in our relationship. "Please don't leave," I tried to sound calm, "before you tell me why . . ."

"You bet your ass I'll tell you why!" Her right foot was one step lower than the left. Still clutching Matt, she began to sway as she tried to turn on the narrow stairs. For a terrible moment I thought they both would tumble backward down the stairs. There were audible gasps from the gallery we'd collected along the hallway.

Then she regained her balance and shakily carried her son up the last two steps. Leora, who'd seen enough, quickly closed her door. One by one the others did the same.

The boy didn't stop screaming. His legs, which had encircled her hips, had lost their grip and were dangling, making each of her steps more awkward as his knees bumped her thighs.

At the threshold of my room she began to yell again. "I'll never let you take him! You—youse people make me sick!"

Then her jutting chin began to tremble and tears spilled from her eyes. She carried Matt in, collapsed into the chair, and broke into sobs, rocking back and forth as she cried. Each forward motion dislodged the screaming child, who grasped the collar of her coat to keep himself from falling. Gradually, as if in slow motion, he slid off her lap until he'd landed on the floor on his back, his eyes staring fixedly at the ceiling while his mouth worked mechanically. The sirenlike wails merged with his mother's sobs.

I was fascinated at seeing them physically separated for the first time. The mother, crying into her hands, seemed not to care that her son had slid from her lap. I edged my chair closer to hers. "What made you think we'd take your son?" I asked.

"I—I tole Frankie last night—this room reminds me about it. It makes me remember an'—an' you remind me, too." Her sobs were muffled, yet anguished. She reached for the tissue box on my desk and swabbed her eyes. Matt's cries now quieted to a softer, babylike sound. She didn't look down, although he lay rocking at her feet.

"The others were older. Me an' Calvin was so—so scared. Calvin was my brother, see. Our father gave us up—only us."

"He gave you up? . . ."

"Oh, he was rotten, the ole man." She rocked as she spoke, clutching her stomach as if she were in pain. "Our mother always saw as we had food—sometimes it wasn't nothin' but biscuits, but she always saw there was somethin' for Calvin an' me t' eat. She usta clean people's houses so's we'd eat. The ole man even beat her to get her money away but she always kept enough so she could feed Calvin an' me. He drank it up, see." This time she rubbed her stomach.

"Then she had the operation—a hectorectomy. But she went right back t' cleanin' houses.

Nobody told us nothin' till she was dead. Me an' Calvin knew she wouldn't have no more babies, but we didn't know she had cancer, too."

"How old were you then?" She brushed her eyes with the back of her hand, then again with the tissues.

"Me an' Calvin wasn't home. She—she died while me an' Calvin was at school. When we got home nobody was there. The next-door neighbor hadda tell us what happened. Our father didn't come back for a week. I—uh—I was eleven, see.

"Then one night some lady came to the door, all dressed up fancy. Says the people our mother worked for took up a collection. An' she left a box with a lotta dollar bills. But the old man, that bum, he took it all away an' drank it up."

She stopped talking and seemed to be lost in thought. I used the moment to put a paper and some crayons on the floor in front of the boy, who was hunched on his knees, whining and rocking himself.

She still looked distant and pensive. "What happened to you and Calvin?" I prompted.

"We didn't have nothin' t' eat at all after that." She continued hesitantly." So Calvin usta go downtown everyday an'—uh—steal us some food. One can under this arm, one can under that arm," she gestured, and paused again. "Finally—the ice chest got so it was almost full. An'—an' then I says, 'Stop, Calvin, 'cause that's enough.' But he didn't never think so.

"Then one day the cops caught him an' brought him home." She sighed, glancing at me very briefly. "When they seen we was alone, they called the state. Some worker come out an' tole us we was state children now, goin' to a real nice home. Ha!" she sneered, her head lowered. "Call that a nice home? The woman who had us kept beatin' on Calvin with a belt 'cause he always wet the bed."

She paused again to hold her hand to her forehead as though she were in pain. "I'd like t' say I brang my brother up," she sighed, "but the honest truth is nobody really did. It—it was so damn sad . . ." She began to pluck the tissue apart.

I felt my own eyes sting with tears because I'd worked with too many foster children who'd been shunted from one home to another. Blinking, I bent forward to see if the child was using the crayons. But he was hunched over the paper, his back toward me. I couldn't tell.

"Calvin was always cryin' that he wanted t' go home," she began again. "An' then just—just exactly one day before Christmas—that's how come Frankie says I tell him this story every year—'cause every Christmas always reminds me of Calvin an' how Calvin started throwin' stones at our foster mother's house. Rocks they was, really. So what does she do? She calls the state worker on both of us. Then that worker comes drivin' up and says we was troublemakers an' we hadda be moved." When she spoke again her tone had changed from sadness to bitterness. "She said that woman had plenty a foster children before an' she never beat any one a them. I says to that worker, 'How come youse always believe the grown-ups and never believe the kids?'"

She leaned toward me, eyes narrowed, as if she expected an answer; but then she continued. "See, that first time I came here, when we seen that other doctor, I began t' remember that state worker looked a lot like you. Then I seen your office an' it looked a lot like hers."

"No wonder you thought we might take Matt . . ." I said.

"That worker—" She stared as though she were envisioning the scene. "That worker—she called a lotta people before anybody said they'd take us. I—I guess that was cause nobody wanted extra kids at Christmastime.

"Finally," she shook her head sadly, "we got in her car, an' she took me an' Calvin for a long, long ride. And—uh—she didn't say nothin' about where we was goin', an' me an' Calvin was too scared t' ask. She kept on drivin' an' we just sat in that car holdin' each other's hands.

"An' then—" Her body began trembling. "Then, when she finally stopped drivin' she says I should wait in the car while my brother meets the new people first. So I sat there thinkin' I'd be gettin' out as soon as she came back, but—but—then," she inhaled a sharp sob, "she came back to the car an'—an' backed it out an' drove away real fast. I screamed and screamed," her voice rose, "that I hadda be with my brother. I hadda stay where Calvin stayed! But she wouldn't stop or nothin'. All she says was her hands was tied. We belonged t' the state an' not t' her."

Tears were rolling down her cheeks. "Then—uh—a long time later she—uh—came back to the people's place where I was livin' then, an'—uh—she took me out in her car again, and drove me back t' the place that looked like this. She says Calvin was inside an' we was allowed t' have a one-hour visit in that room. But Calvin—he acted like he didn't even know me, even though I recognized him right off. He had red hair like me, but his was always curly," she smiled, fingering her own straight hair, "an' the bluest eyes you ever seen.

"So—uh—for awhile Calvin didn't even say nothin'—just stared out the window. An' there really wasn't nothin' t' look at out there. Then, then I ast him if he remembered our real mother, and he began to cry."

Her tears began to flow again. "When the worker says our time was almost up," she paused for a moment, then spoke more softly, "I whispered to Calvin, where did he live? But he didn't know, not even what city. So I tole him my address an' I says, real soft, so the worker wouldn't hear it, 'Lissen Calvin, listen honey . . . '" Suddenly she burst into sobs, and wept openly for several moments. Finally, haltingly, she spoke again. "You— you sneak out an' find me. We can—run away—

together. I—I'm in the last house on Robin's Road. That's where I live.'

"After Calvin left, I ran outta that place. I—I just couldn't hold it in." She dabbed at her eyes with the shredded tissue. "I—uh—I tried tellin' Frankie about it but he says there's no sense thinkin' about things that was so sad. Still I can't help it. I think I'll always remember. It was—it was such a hurtin' experience."

"I know it was hard for you to tell me," I said, "but I'm really glad you did. It helps me understand." She sat rocking, weeping softly, her hand over her mouth.

Again I bent to see the child, touching his shoulder to get his attention. He looked up, rolling his eyes toward the ceiling, carefully avoiding contact with my face. His lips hung open slackly. Chunks of red and purple crayon were stuck to his teeth. Multicolored streams of drool dripped from both corners of his mouth down his chin to the floor. He picked up the last crayon and stuffed it in his mouth, adding to the gob of wax on his tongue.

The paper remained untouched.

Chapter 3

"LIKE I tole you—" she began, as if a week had never passed. Yet there was a subtle change. Matt was whimpering, but it wasn't his usual piercing cry. And though she still seemed to hide behind her son's body, she was angling her head sharply enough now to make her face clearly visible to me.

"Like I tole you," she repeated, "me an' Calvin didn't live together no more, so we didn't see each other again till we was growed up. A couple a times the ole man came t' see me. I guess he seen Calvin, too. One time he says Calvin was in trouble, see, an' they sent him to a institution."

The words came slowly, but she was beginning to glance at me frequently. And her expression was markedly different, more animated, her eyes more lively than before.

"See," she continued, "my brother began takin' things. Stuff he couldn't even use. It was like he hadda grab everything anytime he could." She paused thoughtfully, then continued, "Ya know, I think they got that kid all twisted up inside. Like—like he was, whadya call it, too sensitive." She sat silently a moment, then suddenly erupted. "Ya know, youse workers make me sick!" She shook her fist in the air. "Ya stick people in them foster homes, but ya don't find out what happens to them after that. An' ya don't even care!"

As her anxiety increased, the boy started screaming. Undaunted, she probed into her shoulder bag, and drew out the bottle of milk.

"You stop your tizzy now!" Matt clutched the bottle with both hands, resting his chin on her shoulder, and guzzled eagerly. I shuddered at my own powerlessness to interfere with their strange, inappropriate behavior.

"See," she continued, "I didn't finish no school or nothin', an' the next time I seen Calvin I was gonna have a baby. Maybe the ole man tole him where I lived, 'cause he just showed up at my place and knocked on the door. All I had was five bucks. He was eighteen then, but he was still all twisted inside. I could see he was hurt, an' that hurt me, too. But all he ast was could I give him some money; so I gave him the five bucks. He didn't even say a single thanks. He just turned around an' went away." She paused, and her voice was hollow and distant. "I watched him goin' an' I was thinkin' Calvin couldn't get close to no one no more. Not even t' me.

"Just before I was gonna have the baby, I got a phone call from the county jail. Calvin had a accident, they says. My name was next-a-kin. I didn't understand my brother was dead till the warden says t' claim the body. He says Calvin hung hisself with his bedsheet. That was the accident.

"I guess Calvin felt like me, all empty inside," she said, forlornly. Gently, she'd begun to rock herself and the boy. "I—uh—I was gonna take a bus over t' the jail, but my water broke, see, an' the baby starts comin'. My neighbor hadda call the police. I rode in the backa the police car all alone. I was awful scared. An' Calvin was buried by the state, so I never got t' see his body or nothin'." Tears streamed down her cheeks.

"I had a awful low spirit after that." She pressed her forehead onto her son's shoulder. "I usta cry my eyes out all the time."

"You're still pretty sad," I said quietly. Matt had finished the milk and was drawing air through the nipple.

"Sometimes." She kept her head bowed. "Frankie says I'm like a kid—or also, I'm crazy. He tole me I hafta toughen up. See," her voice became stronger, "youse people shouldn't never stick no kids in foster homes." She paused a moment. "But another thing I wanna ast you . . ." She looked up. I braced myself for another accusation.

31

"See, Frankie buys me an' Matt our clothes sometimes on his way home from work, or sometimes he orders them outta one a them catalogue books. An' I bin wonderin'," her eyes scanned my legs, "where'd you get them pants that fit so good? 'Stead a these cheap things." She plucked at her slacks with disdain. "Know what I mean?—shrink right up your ass everytime you wash 'em."

Every week each person on our staff reviewed his cases in an hourly conference with a supervisor. Leora was mine and I admired her enormously, both professionally and personally.

Having fled Europe in 1939, she still pursued the activities she'd known as a girl in Austria: mountain climbing in the summer, skiing on winter weekends. At sixty-five her body was lean and wiry. Although her hair was gray, her mouth and eyes were edged in kindly crinkles.

Leora had practiced social work from the day she'd received her master's degree at Smith. New students coming to train at our agency often felt rebuffed by her quick and blunt judgments, then lingered to counsel with her as they learned the value of her keenness and integrity.

My hour of supervision was not always impersonal. When Ann, my oldest child, had decided to go to Africa, when Richie became engaged, when Billy announced that his music group was more important than school, and Ellie fell from her horse—Leora listened. Once we met just after she'd learned of the death of a close friend, and she, in turn, shared her feelings.

I saved the Barringers until the end of my hour with her that Thursday, certain that, otherwise, I'd use the entire sixty minutes on them alone. Julie's foster parents were wavering on their commitment to adopt her. I needed Leora's advice on how hard to push. The lesbian couple, each of whom had a child from previous marriages, were having violent fights. Both of their sons were exploding at school. The ten-year-old boy who'd just been released from residential treatment had started a fire in his garage. Finally, I tried to summarize my contacts with Mrs. Barringer and Matt.

"It's an extraordinary situation and your sessions sound exhausting," Leora remarked.

They were, I realized: yet somehow I looked forward to the time I spent with Matt and his mother. I'd never seen a child so primitive. Both his undiagnosed condition and his unknown potential intrigued me.

Leora agreed with Dick that Matt's chances of speaking were poor. "I'm convinced such children are brain damaged, whether or not it shows in tests," she said. "I just don't believe parents do anything so horrendous that they could prevent a normal child from developing speech. Children are natural imitators. This boy has heard his parents talk, and heard radio and television, too.

"If he didn't have some neurological impairment," she shook her head, "the child would be talking today. I don't care what any doctor says . . ."

"That hussy downstairs ain't actin' so snotty." Mrs. Barringer eased herself and her whining son into the now familiar chair. "In fact, she's gettin' real nice."

"It's not Sylvia who's changing," I smiled. "It's you. You're not so afraid."

"Frankie notices it, too," she said, clearly pleased. "He says you an' me can go shoppin' someday. You know, when Matt gets better." While she talked, she pulled the familiar bottle from her purse. Watching her handing it to her six-year-old son reminded me yet again of the irony of her casual assumption that he would surely improve.

"Matt's pretty big for a bottle," I began, intending, finally, to focus on this issue.

"Ya, but you an' me wanna talk an' you know how that kid can scream."

"Mmm." I could certainly agree with that.

"Would he sit by himself to drink it?" I placed the child-sized chair beside them, hoping for just some glimmer of progress.

"Naw," she kicked the chair away. "My son don't sit in no chair. Here—" she drew him from her shoulder and cradled him across her lap as if she were going to feed him. Then, to my surprise, she continued lowering him onto the carpet. He whimpered, but went on sucking, flat on his back, legs drawn up against his stomach in prenatal posture.

"See, I always bin scared."

I was getting used to her habit of jumping back and forth on topics—but was still never entirely prepared for it. Today I had a purpose in trying to keep her thoughts focused. I'd have to present the case to the staff soon and needed to know more about Matt's early development.

"Did you feel the same way—scared—when you were pregnant?" I began.

"Oh sure. I was always real nervous. Mostly it was the idea 'bout gettin' undressed in front of strangers." She began picking at her nails. "I wouldn't go to no doctor before the baby was bein' borned."

I was disappointed to hear this, having hoped there'd be some prenatal records.

"Did you take any medicine while you were pregnant?" It seemed unlikely, since she wasn't under a doctor's care, but it was a question we always asked. Too many subtly damaged children, whose mothers had taken medication during pregnancy, had come to our center for evaluation.

"I wish those obstetricians who prescribe so freely could know what we see years later," our medical director often complained, "children drugged into hyperactivity before birth by mothers who had no warning about taking tranquilizers."

And Mrs. Barringer surprised me by answering yes. "I had that romantic fever, see, when I was a kid. The kind that hurts your heart. An' I was s'posed t' take penicillin so not to get no strep throats again. But I always forget, till I get sick. I took a few a them penicillins 'fore Matt was born, 'cause I had a real bad cold. But I don't even know how many."

Again I remembered the doctor condemning heavy doses of penicillin during pregnancy. "Penicillin competes for oxygen, reducing the supply to the fetus," he'd said. "Women who smoke, drink or take drugs have high-risk babies. Yet it goes on and on. Vitamins are the only safe pill for pregnant women," he'd always insist.

From what she'd said, Mrs. Barringer probably took very little penicillin before Matt was born; yet we'd never know for sure whether medication contributed to her son's condition. She couldn't remember what month of pregnancy she was in at the time. No point in dwelling on what couldn't be changed. I went on with the interview.

"Do you remember the details about his birth? About your labor and his delivery?" I asked.

"Matt come early, see. Cause he started comin' right after I found out about Calvin bein' dead. I run down the hall outside my apartment, screamin', an' that's when the neighbor called the police, an' they took me t' some clinic."

"Do you know the name of the clinic, or the doctor's name?"

"Naw. No special name, just a clinic. No special doctor, just one a them guys in a white suit," she dismissed my question. "But Matt was big. Six pounds, even borned early."

So at least his birth weight was good.

"Did he cry right away when he was born?"

"They hadda knock me out, see, I was fightin' so bad 'bout gettin' put up on that table. I wanted to go right home after I woke up but they gave me some tran—tranquilizers, or somethin', and says I hadda stay till mornin'. New places always scared me. Even here."

I nodded and waited, but she didn't go on. "What happened after you and Matt got home? Was he breast-fed?"

"Are you kiddin'?" She laughed. "That kid usta yell when I tried t' nurse him. So I put him on the bottle an' he wouldn't take nothin' else even after he started gettin' teeth. Fact is, he didn't even like bein' picked up for holdin', so I just left him be. Just left him in bed t' scream. Nasty little thing," she chuckled. "Bangin' his head all the time. He still does it, everytime he has a tizzy."

"Mmm, I know—Can you remember when he began to sit up or stand?" I asked quickly, sensing that her interest was waning.

"Oh, my son was walking good at nine—ten months." She'd begun to rummage through her purse again.

"He didn't never talk, though." She took out a silver perfume container and sprayed herself behind each ear.

"I've thought a lot about his not talking, Mrs. Barringer. It makes me wonder how well he hears."

"Him?" She pointed down at the child. "That kid got ears like a elephant." She laughed. "Knows exactly when his father's truck's turnin' down the road just by the sounda the tires. That's when he starts that nasty tizzy—that bangin' his head 'gainst the door. Matt don't like his father comin' home."

"He doesn't?"

"Scared, see, just like me." She tilted her head to smile down at him as he held the baby bottle to his lips.

"Even when I was a girl, I mean, I was scared. I was in one a them special classes ya know, where you get the same teacher every year. She was nice but I was awful scareda the other kids. They usta call me dummy an' make fun of my clothes. They wasn't so smart either, but the school nurse gave me an' Calvin clothes. We looked different than them other kids. Them kids was right, though," she hunched her shoulders forlornly. "I really am dumb."

Silence.

"Frankie tells me, so I know it's true. He says I can't do nothin' for myself. Ha! I know it too!"

"What can't you do for yourself?"

"He says he brings in all the money. Me, I can't even write my name on one a them stinkin' checks. An' he does all the shoppin' for food an' clothes an' everything. Even takes care of the stinkin' dog. Me—" she hunched her shoulders in an exaggerated shiver. "I'm scared of that nasty thing. But Frankie says we hafta keep it so no one bothers me an' Matt. He says all I can do is cook."

"That's pretty important," I offered.

"Yeah?" She sounded surprised. "Well, my mother taught me cookin' before she died. I liked hangin' aroun' my mother," she said softly. "But see, what Frankie means by 'important' is like takin' care of Matt 'case anything happens to him." She squirmed, looking up again. "Frankie says I oughta learn how to make out them checks. T' pay the bills, I mean. But I'll never spell them words, you know, like how you have to write on checks? I can't spell nothin'.

"I can't drive neither, 'cause I can't read the signs. So Frankie's right. Them kids was right." She picked at her fingernails. "I really am dumb."

Mrs. Barringer's air of resignation disturbed me. "Can you write your name?"

"Gimme a paper." Hunched over, biting her tongue in concentration, she printed N-E-L-L-I-E B-A-R-R-I-N-G-E-R, in large block letters.

I held it up. "Well, that's a start!"

She grinned.

"I'm sure you could learn to write checks," I said. She grabbed the paper from my hand, and looked at it admiringly, but then she was off on another tangent.

"See, I got one sister, a lot older, but she's over in Jersey. I never really heard much from her after our ole man died. An' that's all that's left—just Gloria, 'cept for two brothers."

"Two brothers?"

"Ya, but they ain't no good." She wrinkled her nose in disgust. "One's a jailbird, like Calvin. Frankie says I should forget them all, since I don't mean nothin' to them. But my mother taught us to love each other. Frankie says they don't care about me. But they're all the family I got."

"Do you ever see them?"

"If I could dial I could call them up, see. That's what I'd really like t' do." Writing checks might be helpful, I thought, but dialing could open up another world. It was astounding for me, so often irritated by the telephone, to realize how badly she wanted to use it.

"I wouldn't call everyday, or nothin'. Just Christmas an' holidays to see what they're doin'. Me an' Matt gets lonesome in that house all the time. 'Specially holidays."

"Why stay indoors, Mrs. Barringer? Why not take Matt for a walk?"

"Are you kiddin'? My son's scared a them dogs in the neighborhood."

"Let's see. You're afraid of dogs and so is Matt. Maybe if he saw that you . . ."

"He's afraida them dogs," she said with finality. "But I learned my numbers, see." Another skip in her mental process. She knew the numbers. She could learn to dial but couldn't read the phone book.

"Do you know how to call information?" I asked. She shook her head. I gestured to the phone on the right side of my desk.

"Come watch." She rose slowly from the chair, eyeing the telephone suspiciously.

"Look." I stood beside her. "Information is four-one-one. Now, you do it."

"Four-one-one." She bent over hesitantly, biting her tongue as she located each number.

"Now try it holding the receiver. Ask the number of the County Counselling Center. Come on. Don't be afraid."

"Hey! I can't remember all them words. I'll ask for me an' Frankie's number." She dialed information and spewed out the address. "Three-nineteen Burley Street. Mr. an' Mrs. Frankie Barringer." A pause. "Hey how about that!" She looked at me triumphantly. "Information got it right!"

"Great! Let's try New Jersey information. Then you can call your sister."

As I reached for the phone book, I looked around to check on Matt. Although I had missed seeing him move, somehow he'd managed to get across the room. He was lying on his side spinning the pressure valve on the bottom of the radiator. Suddenly I realized he was barely whimpering—in fact, the whole time we were talking, he'd scarcely made a noise.

We got the area code for New Jersey and after three false starts she succeeded in dialing six-o-nine—five-five-five-one-two-one-two.

"My goodness," she complained. "All them numbers give a person a headache."

I wrote down phone numbers for local information and New Jersey information. "And this is our number here at the Center," I pointed. "If you can't come to your appointment, just let me know. Okay?"

"I'm not gonna call them bums," she said, referring to her sister and family. She folded the paper and tucked it in the back pocket of her bright pink slacks. "Frankie's right. They don't give a damn about me."

The child was lying back by her chair, sucking the empty bottle. Again I'd missed seeing how he'd moved. And she had no idea he'd moved at all.

The next morning brought an inkling of the consequences of teaching her to dial.

"She's called three times," Sylvia handed me the message slips as I was taking off my coat. "She demands to speak to 'Keggie.'"

Mrs. Barringer picked up the receiver on the first ring.

"Where ya been?" she shouted. "I been having a lotta trouble over here. Good thing I didn't wait for your kinda help!"

"What's happened?"

"Ha! Them workers on the road, that's what. I seen them nasty men look at this house when Frankie went to work. They know I'm here alone."

"Did someone bother you?" The thought enraged me.

"Bother me! They're bangin' on them pipes so my water's fulla junk. Information gave me the number an' I tole them stinkin' people off."

"What people, Mrs. Barringer?"

"Them politicians. Down the water company! I says, 'Listen, youse people, my water's red. An' my son drinks that water.' She says t' me, 'I'm only the secretary.'" Mrs. Barringer mimicked the secretary in a high, sarcastic tone. "'You wanna speak to the Water C'missioner?' she asts me. I says, 'Now you just hole on, you politician. I ain't concerned about whose office you park your butt in. My water's red, politician, an' my son drinks this water. So you get off your ass. You fix it for my son!'"

I began to feel like Dr. Frankenstein. What had I unleashed by teaching her to dial?

"Then I called Frankie," she added smugly. "He says he's really prouda me."

I was concerned when I saw "Barringer" scheduled for discussion at Thursday's meeting. Although the six weeks Dick had suggested for evaluation had passed, I still hadn't had six sessions with them. Mrs. Barringer and Matt hadn't come at all for the first, and they'd fled before the second.

I felt nervous at noon when we began to gather in the lunchroom for the meeting. Within minutes Dick Diamond, two psychologists and six of the social workers had arranged themselves in a circle on the hard, metal folding chairs. Inveterate notetakers, they readied their pads, some juggling styrofoam cups of coffee as well.

This meeting was usually the last step in our intake process. The staff would hear the impressions of the worker who'd done the initial interview, discuss the case and formulate a treatment plan. Occasionally the recommendation would be simply to modify the child's program in school. Sometimes the situation was so severe that residential treatment would be considered.

Most meetings ended with a decision for either individual, family or group therapy. We'd begun to avoid labeling one person in a family as the "identified patient." Family therapy was increasingly being recommended as the treatment of choice.

Dr. Diamond nodded to indicate that I would introduce the case. I felt an impulse to let loose, to say "Listen here, all of you, you won't believe this situation—and I really need your help."

Instead, I began formally as everyone expected. After reviewing the background of the case, I explained how the father had brought the boy here to see the doctor.

"That's right, and—uh—those of you who haven't seen him—uh—have probably heard him." Dick seemed disconcerted. "The boy was screaming when his mother carried him into my office and didn't stop for a moment. It sounded, as some of you know, like the cry of a newborn baby.

"I couldn't physically separate the mother

and child or accomplish anything with either. They seemed to be hiding behind each other. Finally, I sent them downstairs and tried to question the father alone, using the Vineland Social Maturity Scale to get some idea of the boy's personal and social development."

Dick Diamond's self-consciousness diminished as he made the presentation. Although he kept his gold-rimmed reading glasses on, he began to speak without referring to his notes.

"From what Mr. Barringer said, the child accomplishes nothing above the two-year level. He doesn't speak, isn't toilet trained, won't feed himself and has never been with other kids.

"One mystery here is why these parents didn't come for help before. The mother, like the child, is obviously terrified. I see them locked in by mutual needs and fears.

"I tried to explore the father's role—whether he even realizes the level on which his son is functioning. I started to point out to him the difference between permanent retardation and functional retardation, where the child's potential might be higher. His only comment was, 'When you people get my son to act right, you'll see how smart he really is.'"

Leora and I exchanged wry smiles across the room.

"The father was an orphan," Dick continued, "raised in an institution until his early teens. He attended school through seventh grade and now is in charge of the equipment at the Coolidge Square Laundry.

"Every evening he does the shopping for all their food and supplies, serving as their only link to the outside world."

"Why?" someone murmured.

"If we understood the parents' behavior we might have the key to the boy's condition. I can only say that when the father describes his wife's dependency he sounds more gratified than upset."

There were muffled murmurs in the room.

"What about *her* background?" one of the women asked.

"Mrs. Craig can answer that better than I."

I summarized what I knew of Mrs. Barringer's childhood, her pregnancy and delivery, her sketchy information on the boy's developmental history. I described the confusing mixture of insight and limitation when she spoke of herself and her son.

"It's become clear to me that she derives benefits from her son's deviancy, which allows her to remain housebound, protected from the world she's found too frightening to face.

"Yet, although she was originally terrified, once we got started she's kept the appointments faithfully. Ceil Black has been driving them here. The mother never speaks on the rides, just holds the boy who, until recently, cried constantly."

At first, no one spoke when I finished. Finally Doug, one of the social workers, took a swig of coffee and leaned toward the doctor. Young, intense, only recently out of graduate school, Doug looked intrigued by the case. "Did the mother say anything at all to you, Dick?"

"Hmm." Dr. Diamond held his chin reflectively. "Just one comment. She said she wanted us to 'serve' her son."

"I wonder whether she meant serve or *observe*," Leora commented.

The psychiatrist shrugged.

"And that's all the diagnostic material? No tests?" Doug challenged. Shaking his head, he crossed his arms and stretched his lanky legs.

"Doug," Dr. Diamond smiled patiently, "this boy is far from ready for testing. But we don't need scores to confirm his retardation, whether it's permanent or functional." He paused. "I suppose one could argue that he's clearly organic—brain damaged for undetermined reasons."

Leora nodded in agreement.

"But," he continued, "we can't discount the impact of the parents' bizarre behavior on the boy's emotional and intellectual growth . . . I don't think it's possible to pinpoint the cause from what we know so far. It makes me think of Itard's case, you know, the Wild Boy of Aveyron."

Dr. Diamond's digression, I felt, was designed to reduce the tension between himself and Doug.

"Itard worked with the boy for years, assuming his idiocy was due to lack of social stimulation. I suppose it's the first recorded case of autism. So, let's hope we have more success with this case." He paused again. "Well, I won't digress any further." I saw him glance at Doug. "Surely you have comments on the case we've heard today."

Doug squirmed uncomfortably. "I do. In my opinion it's completely inappropriate for this agency. Our first obligation is to the more normal kids on the waiting list. This is no reflection on either Dr. Diamond or Eleanor, but our clinic can't become a dumping ground for kids no one knows what else to do with."

Dr. Diamond paused to light his pipe. "Why not?" Eyes narrowed, he looked at Doug.

Doug flushed. "Because we'd have a counselling center full of undiagnosed, functionally retarded kids."

"No other agency in this area," the psychiatrist drew on the pipe, "has the kind of set-up we do here. We've made our team method work for diagnoses as well as for treatment. We all know the kind of run-around parents get with a kid like this. Let's extend ourselves so it won't happen to these frightened people."

"Of course, we should make exceptions," Doug replied. "But not when the extent of retardation is as severe as it seems in this case, regardless of cause."

Others around the room looked helplessly from Doug to Dr. Diamond, aware that their disagreement masked a struggle for power between the two that had become increasingly tense in the past months.

Doug cleared his throat and plunged on, his long bony fingers tapping nervously on his knee. "I'll say it again. We owe it to the community to treat the children we were established to serve." He sounded irritated. "We're not an agency for the retarded—regardless of what factors contribute to the retardation—whether it's functional or temporary or whatever you want to call it. God, that kid upsets the whole place with his screaming. Why should any of us be subjected to that? They can't even wait in the waiting room like everybody else."

One of the social workers who rarely spoke at meetings looked at him timidly. "But Doug, listen, maybe Dr. Diamond is right. I think sometimes, especially for a mental health agency, we let ourselves be bound too rigidly by criteria." She wrung her hands as she spoke.

"These parents had enough confidence to bring the child to us." The woman continued more firmly. "And surely from what Eleanor says this isn't the kind of mother who's able to go on looking for help. If we won't help them now, the child may never have another chance.

"It sounds to me as though she'd almost prefer staying locked in that house, and we can't let her do that. We don't really understand the dynamics here; but she's willing to come, so let's see whether anything can be accomplished."

Some decision had to be made. We were in

the last ten minutes of the hour. Dr. Diamond looked around, then broke the heavy silence. "Why don't we work with them at least until the child is testable? When we get an EEG and a thorough neurological examination we'll know whether to refer them elsewhere.

"I suppose we could argue now whether this is brain damage, autism, or childhood schizophrenia," he continued. "But why? Until we have more information we'd just be spinning theories. While we work to bring him to the point of being ready for testing, we might put the boy on medication to see whether it helps him become calmer, less afraid.

"It's certainly clear these parents need counselling—regardless of the diagnosis. We'd also want to know more about the father and why he tolerates such dependency. But the treatment will have to focus on the mother. If we want to reach the boy, we'll have to begin with her."

"Don't look at me," Doug murmured, eyes downcast.

"Eleanor often sees our younger patients," Leora said. "This child certainly functions at a younger level, and she and the mother already have some relationship. I feel she should continue."

Last chance to object, I warned myself, aware that silence now amounted to consent. "Okay, I want this case, though I'm not sure why."

"So they're yours!" Dr. Diamond rose and handed me the folder.

"She can have them," Doug muttered, hurrying out of the room.

Chapter 4

EIL Black's office called the next Wednesday to say she was ill and wouldn't be able to bring the Barringers, so I started to use their scheduled time to bring my files up to date. But, even with the door closed, there was no mistaking the cries in the hall.

"Ha!" The door was banged open against the wall. She stood grinning over the head of the boy, whose crying had softened. "Thought you'd have your sneaky little time to yourself?"

"I'm really surprised you're here! I heard Mrs. Black was sick."

"Sure. Me an' Matt took a cab."

"You did?" I was astonished that she cared

enough to come to the Center on her own. "Hey, that's really great."

"Ya, well it ain't so great what the cab driver says about youse people. He's been in this place with his own kid, see. Says all youse people here are crazy yourselves. Just wantin' t' know all that bedroom stuff." She dropped into the chair, Matt's legs straddling her lap, his face to the wall.

"Do you believe the things he said?" I frowned, trying to look and sound as serious as she.

"I tole him my worker never ast me none of that business yet. You never did—'bout if Frankie's gettin' much. But Frankie ain't got no complaints, ya know."

She changed Matt's head from its resting place on her left shoulder to her right. Though he hadn't stopped crying, he allowed her to move him about without resisting. Her whole face was visible to me, and the feeling of her using him as a shield between us was gone.

"Hey." She thumped her hand on my desk emphatically. "'Member how you taught me to dial? The phone, I mean. Well," she gloated, "I called up my sister, Gloria, see. But she got that effilefsy, ya know. An' she gets into them fits, so she says she don't feel good enough t' talk. I says call me back, hon."

Absentmindedly she patted her son's back. "That bum didn't call me for three days. An' when she did, she collected the call. That means me an' Frankie has t' pay. I know Frankie's gonna be awful mad, but I hafta talk to somebody . . . " Her voice trailed off wistfully.

"You're feeling pretty lonesome," I said.

She nodded silently a moment. But when she spoke, her voice had resumed its stridency. "That bum tole me she's on welfare now. Doin' a lot of runnin', ya' know. Bringin' lotsa men t' the house. I says, 'Gloria, with your kids right there?' She don't care. I tole her that ain't right."

Head bowed, she kept her eyes lowered. "An' she says my brother's kids is all in foster homes now. My brother—he ain't no good either. He's still in jail." She sighed.

"You look sad when you talk about them. It seems you and Frankie want more for Matt than they're giving their kids. And you're really working at it. Just the things I'm hearing today are such big changes. You're making phone calls, taking a taxi . . ."

"I like comin' here, see." She looked directly at me. "Makes me kinda glad really, you teachin' me how to help my son."

I looked at the back of his head bobbing rhythmically as he cried softly, routinely, continually. "Wa-wa wa-wa." The bizarre refrain had become a constant background to our conversations. Listening to it, I knew I had yet to help this boy. Her words now meant that I could try.

I knew exactly where to start. Doug had pointed it out at the staff meeting. They were the only patients not required to stop in the waiting room. By protecting them, I continued to limit their exposure to new situations. There could be no more exceptions for the Barringers. Her coming by cab meant she was ready to see more people, to be treated "normally."

"We're just beginning to help Matt, Mrs. Barringer. We'll work on one thing at a time, till he's ready for the next. The biggest step was your bringing him here. It shows that *you're* not frightened, and that's important for Matt. Children can sense their parents' feelings, even when we try to hide them. I think the next thing you two should do is get used to seeing a few more people." She immediately drew back, her eyes wide—alarmed.

"Don't be afraid," I smiled. "I just mean here—in the waiting room. I think you and Matt are ready to stop there first, instead of rushing up here. Let's go look in together, so you can see what it's like."

"You gotta be kiddin'." She wrapped both arms tightly around her son. He screamed louder than before. "My son an' I ain't never sittin' with them snobs. What am I supposed t' say? It's a nice day out?" She paused, glaring angrily at me. Then her voice softened. "I don't even know what t' wear!"

"You look fine. There's nothing to worry about. I just want you to practice sitting there with me today."

I stood up, but Mrs. Barringer had slumped forward. "Aaah—aaah," she groaned. With her hands under his body, she eased Matt to the floor. "Oh, aaah, it hurts." She clutched her abdomen.

I thought she'd panicked at the thought of going downstairs. But beads of moisture were breaking out on her forehead and upper lip. Her face was drained of color.

Both hands on her stomach, she rocked and moaned. "It hurts. Aaah."

Matt began to screech, and I was frightened too. "Can I help? What's wrong?"

"My—my—aaah—'pendix," she panted. "Been, oooh—been hurtin' a few months." Matt was lying on his back screaming tearlessly, his arms and legs flailing.

"Let me call a doctor . . ."

"Uh-uh. No!" Gradually she straightened up her body. "It's—it's better now," she murmured. "See, I know it's 'pendix cause Frankie says he can tell. But—I—I can't go to no hospital yet." She blotted her face with a tissue. "Not til you get Matt straightened out." I was stooping, half-kneeling in front of her to hear above the racket the boy was making. She massaged her stomach. "You know I can't leave my son with nobody."

"That's not true," I said. "Your health is too important to him for you to take chances."

"I know." Her head was bowed, chin on her chest. "I know they could bust. They been hurtin' worse lately. But my son can't be with nobody 'cept me."

Suddenly Matt, still on his back, began

pounding on his forehead with alternating fists. Thump-thump. Thump-thump. It was painful to watch him attack himself.

"See what I mean?" She looked up. "There he goes with one of his tizzies."

He flipped over onto his stomach, raised himself to crawling position and started whacking his forehead against the tiled floor. She was better, but in no condition to struggle with him. I placed my hands on his shoulders, pulled him to a sitting position, his back against my legs, then caught hold of his wrists.

"No Matt. No hurting. I won't let you hurt yourself."

He snapped his head to the right and sank his teeth into the back of my hand. The pain was agonizing and I instantly let go. He leapt up, ran to my desk, and tossed all the folders, papers, the clock and the telephone onto the floor.

Then he dashed to the closet I'd never realized he'd noticed, yanked open the door and hurled all the dolls, soldiers, games, clay, and crayons back over his shoulders. I was frozen, unable to move as I watched this display of initiative. I'd never seen him act on his own before—not even walk!

Squadrons of toys sailed through the air, smashing each other as they landed. When the shelves were empty, and the room devastated, he backed out from the closet and began kicking the dolls against the walls.

"That's him in his tizzy." She shook her head admiringly. "What he done to your closet he does to my 'frigerator every day."

Suddenly he dropped down on his hands and knees, fracturing a plastic checkerboard with his weight. Now with a high-pitched, sirenlike cry, he smashed his head on a mound of assorted toys and game pieces. Each time he got up to pummel himself again, more bits of shattered crayon stuck to the rising welts on his forehead.

Was this his response to his mother's pain? Had he understood when she mentioned leaving him? Or was it a bizarre coincidence that some inner fantasy drove him to punish himself at this moment? I chose to believe he'd understood.

"Mother's okay, Matt. You felt so bad you wanted to hurt yourself, but it's okay—she's fine now."

I knelt directly before him and was able to hold his hand without a struggle. Gradually he stopped screaming and he started to rock and moan. I wasn't sure whether my words would comfort him, or trigger another tantrum, until I felt his hand pull mine toward his stomach. When my hand, cupped over his, touched his abdomen he groaned as she had.

"Mother's stomach's all right, Matt. You're both all right now." I could feel his muscles relax and he leaned a little closer. His cry diminished to a humming, almost purring sound. I felt terribly drawn to this sad little boy who had shown me he understood more than I'd realized. I wondered how his cheeks would look if they could play outdoors, if his eyes weren't sunken in bluish hollows.

Then, abruptly, his mother's harsh voice jarred the moment.

"Saaay—what're you two lovebirds doin' down there?" The words oozed sarcasm. "Make a person feel left out." Now the hurt cracked through.

It was her turn. Looking directly at her, I patted Matt's hand a last time as I withdrew my own. He whimpered, but his tantrum was ended.

"So what's this about the waitin' room? What am I supposed t' wear t' keep them snobs from starin'?" She unwrapped a stick of gum, folded it and stuffed it in her mouth.

"Now let's see." I scrutinized her carefully, to acknowledge her concern. "That white blouse with the black slacks looks fine. No problem with your clothes at all. But I'm certainly worried about your health. Are you sure you're all right? Won't you please go see a doctor?"

"You must think I'm some kinda baby. Lissen." She wrapped her hand around my wrist. "Don't say nothin' t' Frankie. He's comin' next week, like you ast, on his vacation. So don't go talkin' 'bout my 'pendix. Watch out what you say behind my back." She let go of my arm, sat back and snapped the chewing gum.

Frank Barringer reached for the pack of

Marlboros in the shirt pocket of his green uniform. "I been worried about my son for a long time," he said. "A fella where I work, Joey Conte, the one who tole me t' call youse up, has trouble with his kid, too. He says it sounds like my son got a 'deep-seated emotional problem.' Now I'm not so sure I'd call it that." He rolled his head back and exhaled a series of carefully executed smoke rings.

"What's your feeling about his problem?" I asked.

"Look," he threw his palm up, "when I called the first time I was really lookin' for someone who could help me with my wife. But don't tell her that. I wanted someone to show her how to take care of my son, teach her how to make him mind. The kid would be all right if she'd just control him. Instead she spoils him rotten." He leaned forward, jabbing the cigarette inches from my face. "At home, she don't even make that kid keep his clothes on at all. He runs around naked like an animal.

"Now this week's my vacation." He cupped cigarette ash in his stubby hand. "An' I was hopin' she'd let me take them out, just for a ride. But she says no. I've gotta get them outta the house, even kinda gradual like. The way things stand, she don't let me bring anyone home or take them out, ever.

"So you ask me what I think? My son don't hafta behave. He don't hafta talk. Not for her. Just cryin' gets him anything he wants. She answers to that."

Mr. Barringer stared down at the glowing tip of his cigarette, then raised his face and spoke thoughtfully.

"If you wanna know the truth, it ain't just the kid's got a problem. I see myself losin' out with my wife, see, and it's affectin' my marriage."

I felt a deep weariness in this man, as if he'd lived in that face and body too hard, too long. Yet there was a youthful cockiness about his greased-back hair, his pride in producing perfect smoke rings.

"I wonder why it's so hard for Mrs. Barringer to let go of Matt," I ventured. "Or even to let you help with him."

He ground the cigarette out in the ashtray and reached for another. "The way I figure," he said and inhaled deeply, "everyone's always took advantage of my wife. She's been cheated and lied to so much she just can't face life no more. She don't trust anybody, and far as the kid's concerned that includes me.

"It's real strange though," he said pensively. "I had the same kinda experience growing up and it made me tough. Ran away from a boys' home the day I turned thirteen. Christian Charities place, ever heard of that?"

I nodded.

"Ha!" he laughed bitterly. "I couldn't take their kinda charity—dished out on the end of a belt. Not all of them, see. Some was kind, but that birthday I took my last beatin'—from them folks at least. I climbed out the winder after dark and started washin' dishes in a diner the next day. After that it was hard knocks all the way. Joined the merchant marine two years later and traveled all around South America on one of them freighters. When I got tired of travelin' I ended up drivin' a milk route, then switched to a laundry. That's how I met Nellie, pickin' up laundry for the place where I used to work.

"Ya know," he said as he rubbed his forehead, "I still can't understand how all them rough times made me wanna fight back." There was a tightness in his voice now, a hint of anger too long controlled. "But Nellie, having it tough just made her want to quit. I dunno. Maybe—maybe it's because she's a woman. Still," he looked up, "it makes me feel kinda good to take care of them."

"You like to have them need you." Perhaps at last I'd understand just how much he himself needed their dependency.

"Well, it ain't exactly that—at least not anymore. At first I guess I liked it, but now my son's gettin' too big for his mother's kind of babyin'. If he don't start soon, I'm afraid he'll never learn nothin'. And I worry about if something happens to me. Where would Nellie be? She can't even take care of herself."

"I agree with you, Mr. Barringer, and I really think she's trying to become more independent now. I'm starting to see some changes. I wonder if you do."

"See, I've always been dreamin' about driving down to Atlantic City for a vacation. I don't think she'll ever change enough for that. But like I did tell her, after you straighten out the boy, you two can go shoppin'. You know, the way women like doin' that kinda stuff. I thought you'd maybe show her how to buy a coat or somethin'. I'll give her fifteen bucks or so to spend. But all that's only when my son gets better." He looked me in the eye.

"I don't want you to think I have some magic," I said, "to make problems disappear." I was concerned about his expectations being so completely unrealistic. "You see, some children who haven't learned to talk by Matt's age never do. The ones who improve usually start very slowly. It will be a long time, and it will take a lot of effort from both of you, from all of us, to help Matt change. I wonder just what you'd like to see for Matt, Mr. Barringer. What do you want for him?"

"I don't expect he'll ever become a manager," he patted the title embroidered on his shirt. "And I don't intend to push my son. There's really only two things I want from him. First," he sat back and held up his index finger, "in case of war, if called upon to do so, he's gotta have the courage to serve his country well. Second," and now two fingers were raised, "I do expect him to sleep with women. It would be very hard on a father, you know, to have a homosexual son."

During May and June, Matt's behavior changed noticeably. Each session began the same way: crying, clinging to his mother. But now, and it began earlier each week, he would slide from her lap to explore the room. At first he crawled around, returning quickly to her arms. Then he was walking, venturing to the closet and staying longer and more frequently each time.

As the weeks passed, his anxiety lessened. His whining gradually became a contented drone. His mother heard the difference. "I couldn't stand that whinin', that awful howling Matt usta do. He's better now."

Yet when I spent time with him, showing him a puzzle or how to spin a top, her own voice rose frantically. She let me know that Matt could roam as long as she alone had my attention.

Ignoring him cost me dearly. In seconds he'd clear off every shelf in the closet, dumping marbles, puzzles, checkers, dollhouse furniture into a pile that took half an hour to sort when they'd left. I tried to prepare the room for his arrival, storing games in the hall closet—and was startled that he remembered what had been there and went into a violent tantrum when he found some boxes missing. He dropped to the floor and rolled around screaming, pounding his fists against his temples. I couldn't hold onto him without getting kicked. Words of comfort caused him to shriek even louder.

His mother enjoyed his tantrums, using the

free moments to light a cigarette, a new activity for her. "There goes his tizzy." She'd smile with pride at her writhing son.

They came regularly by cab now, an independence we chose to foster, although Ceil was willing to continue driving. One Wednesday Mrs. Barringer talked about a new cab driver.

"Honest, this one said nice things about this place. He wasn't the nasty one. And besides, Frankie says so what if youse people do wanna talk bedroom stuff sometimes? Sex ain't dirty if it's placed right, ya know."

She'd even begun stopping by Sylvia's desk to pay, as other patients did. Our fees were based on last year's income, eight-tenths of one percent of taxable income. Because the Barringers got a rebate, their hour-long sessions cost the minimum rate: one dollar and fifty cents. Gradually, I'd embarked upon the monumental task of teaching her to deal with some of the manifestations of Matt's condition. I began by having her dictate a list of his most troublesome behavior, agreeing that we would approach one problem at a time.

"Well, I sure wish he wouldn't empty out my 'frigerator, spillin' all that salad oil on all them walls. An' I don't like him breakin' all my dishes, 'cause he does it deliberate-like on the floor. What I mind most is his peein' on the couch. An' when me an' Frankie put one a them plastic covers on the seats Matt got all the eggs and mustard outta the 'frigerator and stirred that stuff up on top a that couch. Broke a whole dozen eggs."

When she finished, I read back the list of problems and we agreed to concentrate first on toilet training. But my suggestions always failed. Each week she'd report triumphantly, "I tried what you said and it didn't work."

But other things *were* working. They now stopped in the waiting room. Matt still cried there, but she no longer claimed that people stared or gave her nasty looks because she didn't know what to wear. "I figure," she said one day, "they wouldn't be there theirselves if there wasn't somethin' wrong with them. I mean, they ain't no better than me an' my son."

I often felt drained after their visits, but it wasn't the boy's crying or his messes that bothered me most. It was Mrs. Barringer's stories of the havoc in which her family had lived and how this havoc had been inflicted on others that began to haunt me: endless, hopeless tales of welfare, foster care and jail. Each week there'd been another call to her sister in New Jersey.

"Gloria says her daughter's sleepin' with some guy. That kid's eleven years old. He's thirty-five. I tole her that ain't right. An' he hurt her too. Knocked half her teeth out 'fore shootin' up his arm with that dope stuff. Crashed into a tree, see. An' the woman in the back seat's critical. Got three kids. He never had no license neither. I asked

Gloria when she's gettin' her kid's teeth fixed. She don't wanna bother about nothin'. I says what're ya gonna do? Put her in a freak show?

"Yesterday Gloria says my brother DeWitt, the one just got outta jail, got locked in one of them nut-houses. He was runnin' around without no pants in one a them ladies' rooms down the park. I called the nut-house, see, to find out how DeWitt's been doin'. Them rotten punks say no information 'cept to the wife. Myself, I don't buy DeWitt's really crazy. But I think he is disturbed. Like Calvin.

"Well I found out DeWitt's wife's not gonna call about him at all. She dumped all them kids in foster homes just so she could live with some tramp. In one room. My sister Gloria says, in other words, it's just a shack job."

One Friday at six I found myself reading case records. I'd come to realize that I stayed late on the days it was hardest to make the transition between the clinic and my home, between patients and family, lest one intrude upon the other.

Then Doug, in a worn gray suit, appeared in the doorway. "You still working, too?" He sat on the arm of the chair, his briefcase in his hand. "God, I'm having trouble leaving tonight. Just saw a kid—thirteen—who threatens to jump off the roof of her school. I decided not to hospitalize her—not now, at least, so I gave her my home phone to call me anytime—day or night. She promised not to hurt herself all weekend."

We sat in silence a moment, depressed by the terrible impact of one child's despair.

"I know it's going to haunt me till I see her," Doug said slowly. "And tomorrow's my own kid's second birthday.

"I don't know what's going on." He sighed, not looking up. "Every year we're getting more and more severely disturbed kids. Sometimes I feel I have to guard myself against getting sucked into their depressions. It reminds me of training in the state hospital. Huh!" he laughed bitterly. "At least we were pretty sure of ourselves there: We were the ones who carried the keys."

Chapter 5

WITH a lot of encouragement, Mrs. Barringer kept an appointment for Matt to see a neurologist on the sixth of June. The doctor's report arrived the last week of the month: results, inconclusive. I was disappointed, but not surprised.

"Your patient, Matt Barringer, was referred, as you know, for extreme behavioral problems.
. . .

"There have been no past diagnostic studies, although the mother states that she understands that the child has not developed as he should. Neurological examination revealed an alert hyperactive child who cried constantly throughout the examination.

Mentation—The child shows no evidence of any speech and is constantly moving about and crying.

Motor—Gait appears grossly normal. All extremities move well. Tone is normal. There are no apparent cerebellar abnormalities.

Reflexes—Deep tendon reflexes are fairly brisk throughout. There are no Babinski signs.

Sensory—The child responds well all over to pin prick.

Cranial Nerves—Pupils are equal, round and reactive. Fundi are not well visualized. Extra-ocular muscles appear intact. There is no nystagmus or facial weakness. Tongue is midline. Hearing seems normal.

General—No bruits are heard in the head or neck. There is no apparent tenderness on percussion of the skull or spine. The child's head appears possibly slightly small, no measurement was done at this time. Fontanels are closed.

Formulation—At this time it would seem as if Matt is a severely retarded nonverbal child. At this point it would be fruitless to obtain further diagnostic studies until the child is more controllable. I have started him on Mellaril concentrate 10 m.g. t.i.d. and will increase this dosage in the future if necessary. If and when we can achieve better control, EEG, skull films, funduscopic examination and possible amino acid screen will be obtained.

"In conclusion, at this time it is difficult to say whether the child's functioning at a level of severe retardation is due to cerebral damage, metabolic problems or to emotional disturbance. During the interview it was noted that the mother's affect is quite inappropriate. No previous attempt had been made to evaluate Matt neurologically, although he has obvious gross difficulties.

"Thank you for sending Matt to me for neurological consultation."

Leora handed the neurologist's report back to me. "His comment about Mrs. Barringer's inappropriate affect is interesting. We sometimes overlook emotional problems in persons of limited intellect, though God knows even retardation doesn't protect people from mental illness.

"Yet his suggestion that Matt's retardation might be due to emotional disturbance just doesn't satisfy me in terms of speech. I still say there has to be neurological damage, whether or not it shows in examination."

Her words reminded me of a boy whose family I'd seen some time ago. "Then what about David Coddington?" I asked.

"But he was different," Leora said. "His talking stopped after the child had shown he had the physical capacity to speak. We have no proof of that with Matt."

After Leora left, I sat thinking of my many hours with David Coddington's parents. Actually, the family had come because they were concerned about the brother, Paul, who'd begun to worry them by talking less and less. He often closeted himself in his bedroom for hours at a time.

Gradually, the story of David, Paul's older brother, unfolded. He'd been a beautiful baby, a sturdy, fair-haired toddler. Mr. Coddington, a lawyer, loved playing with his firstborn. Each morning while the child watched him shave, his father entertained him—singing songs from *Man of La Mancha,* which he'd performed in college.

To his delight the child began to sing along. By three, David echoed his father's words. "I am I, Don Quixote . . ." they'd sing, ". . . my destiny calls and I go . . ."

At three and a half, just after Paul was born, David changed. He'd lie for hours watching the wheels of his tiny truck turn as he rolled it. "An engineer, like his uncle," they'd said. But the once joyful boy grew more and more subdued.

"Deep in thought," they told each other.

"Could be jealous of his brother," the pediatrician said. "He'll shape up soon."

They almost ignored the baby, in their effort to cajole his older brother, David. But even the morning songs were different. David participated less and less. A phrase here and there. Finally he was only humming. By five, he'd stopped even that. David no longer talked at all.

"He could have a brain lesion," the neurologist suggested. "But there's nothing we can do. If there's pressure, it doesn't show on any tests."

The family subjected itself to psychiatric investigation. Any dark family secrets? Some reason for reduced motivation or depression on David's part? Had he suffered from shock or an accident? No evidence of child abuse or parental rejection.

"Childhood psychosis," one psychiatrist insisted. "We can offer no clear-cut reason or cure."

At six, David went to classes for the "trainable retarded," but his teachers couldn't reach him. He became less manageable as he grew. There were rampages of smashing things, black days when he isolated himself in his room. Once he tore all the stuffing from his mattress. When he was eleven, his mother could no longer handle him. The parents finally had to put David in residence at the regional mental health center.

Then his brother Paul, age nine, gradually began to regress, withdrawing from contact with his family and friends. With help, Paul revealed to us and came to understand that he was testing his parents. Would he, too, be sent away? He was desperate to know. Once his parents realized that his behavior was a symptom of his anxiety, they were able to reassure him, and Paul improved very fast.

But I remember wishing they'd come to the

Center before David was institutionalized. The feelings could have been worked through then, preventing Paul's regression.

I saw them last after they'd visited the mental health center to celebrate David's twelfth birthday. They'd brought him a portable stereo and just one record—*Man of La Mancha.*

David, they told me, sat quietly.

"He likes music," his caseworker at the center assured them.

"I am I, Don Quixote . . ." the record played.

But David gave no sign to his anxious father that this song had any special significance.

Leora was right. David had been able to talk, though no one was sure what made him stop. Matt had yet to prove he could say a word.

I followed Mrs. Barringer up the stairs, the ever-present teacher in me eager to make the most of each moment. As I'd done before I counted out the steps, hoping Matt would notice. "One, two, three . . ."

But I finished with a sense of futility. Again, no glimmer of understanding in Matt's hooded eyes. As soon as she sat down, the boy squirmed off her lap and went to the closet shelf where wooden puzzles were stacked. I expected to hear them drop, but Matt surprised me by taking just one and sat on the floor to remove the five puzzle parts that formed an apple.

"That doctor—" His mother paused to blow out the flame from her cigarette lighter. "That one you sent us to," she said as she tucked the lighter in the pocket of her stiff-looking jeans studded with silver nailheads.

"Know what he 'spected? He's nuts, that guy. 'Spected my son t' lie on his 'zamination table. Tried t' grab the kid right outta my arms. My son got away." She broke into a grin. "Ran that doctor all over the room," she gloated. "Poor little kid, kept tryin' t' get t' me.

"Then know what he says? How come I can't make him mind?" She mimicked the stern neurologist and her own angry reply. "I says, 'You gotta be kiddin'! My son ain't no guinea pig t' go on your table.'"

Matt dropped the puzzle and clambered back onto his mother's lap, burying his head against her shoulder.

"Then what'd he ask me?" She bit her lower lip, and closed her eyes. "Oh yeah, I remember. Did I enjoy my son? Now what kinda question's that? What does that guy 'spect? 'Course I enjoy my son,' I says. 'Whether he's nasty or not, I enjoy him.' Why should I lie to that doctor?

"After that, I caught the doctor 'servin' me without really lookin', like I wouldn't see his sneaky little peeks.

"Know what I bin doin'? Ever since we went there I bin tryin' it at home. 'Servin' Matt while he don't know I'm watchin'. I tole Frankie it seems like

Matt's tryin' t' shake it off, whatever's wrong with him.

"See, somebody down the Coolidge Laundry tole Frankie a person's system changes every seven years. Like some people get a seven-year itch. At least my son ain't got that. But Matt's the right age. Me an' Frankie think his system's probably changin'."

"I wonder about the medicine the doctor prescribed . . ."

"Oh," she interrupted, "Frankie went and got that description filled, see, an' Matt really liked it. But Frankie heard an article on TV about drugs bein' bad for kids, turnin' them into 'ad-dicks', so we threw that stuff down the toilet."

I wouldn't argue. Not now, anyway. If they gave him medicine reluctantly they wouldn't do it faithfully, and the prescription would be worthless. Matt tried to climb off her lap, taking her coffee with him, but the hot liquid splashed on his hands. He dropped the cup and screamed.

"My God!" She grabbed him in her arms. "Where's the bathroom? Where's some water for my son?"

"Mrs. Barringer, I don't think it was hot enough to hurt him . . ."

But she was running down the hall and disappeared behind the bathroom door. Moments later she carried him back, his hands wrapped in damp paper towels.

"At least my son don't say no dirty words."

She lowered him gently to the floor, close to his puzzle. "My sister's kid, he yells that real dirty word right in the phone while I'll be payin' for the call. I says, 'Gloria wash out his mouth with soap.' But she don't do nothin'. Even if he's hurt," she looked at Matt fondly, "my son don't never say those words."

Or any others, I thought sadly.

Sniffling, Matt unwrapped his hands and picked up the puzzle. He was now paler than ever, his eyes lost in the round purple shadows.

Mrs. Barringer kept talking. I watched with pleasure as he reconstructed the puzzle without hesitation. A severely retarded child would be struggling with those spacial relationships. I couldn't resist going to the closet for a harder puzzle, responding to his mother over my shoulder. Matt reached up, took the puzzle from my hands and quickly put in the ten pieces that formed a firetruck.

Delighted, I handed him another.

His mother ran reports of one incident into another, paying no attention to her son's success. "Ya know Gloria an' her kids is all on welfare now. So I called up them welfare people to get me some money, too. An' they says I don't qualify. Ha! I really tole them people off.

"Who do they think they are? Payin' for tramps like Gloria, an' not for me? Least they should make her get a hectorectomy, I tole them, so they won't be paying for no more babies . . ."

Matt finished the puzzle, picked up the empty coffee cup and carried it to his mother.

"What is it?" The interruption annoyed her. "Is it more coffee? Oh no! You already spilled it!"

He began to tug at her sleeve.

Visibly perturbed, she pushed his hand away and began to talk more rapidly. But Matt wouldn't stop. He held the cup to her face, again pulling at her arm.

"Let's see if he'll settle for water," I suggested.

"You can take him. Not me." She looked angry.

I opened the door and he ran ahead to the bathroom. He was filling the cup with water by the time I reached him. Then very carefully he turned and cautiously carried it back to the room.

But his mother was gone. Matt dropped the cup, spilling the water all over his pants. He ran to look in the closet and, not finding her there, began to throw all the toys, cartons of clay and puzzles across the room.

Then he dashed to her empty chair, hurled the two cushions onto the floor, jumped on them, kicked them, turned the frame of the chair upside down, swept everything off my desk, tore across the room and began pounding his head against the wall.

"Stop!" I yelled. Twisting, kicking, he eluded me as I tried to grab him.

Where could she have gone? The phone was

on the floor, buried under my papers and books. I pulled at the cord to retrieve it and call downstairs. But Matt was streaking across the room, heading directly toward the window.

"No!" I was shaking as I grabbed his shirt-tail just when his hand smashed the glass. We both stood trembling, but the window was only cracked.

Whining shrilly, he let me examine his hand. He wasn't even scratched, but I felt weak.

"Ha!" Hands on her hips, she stood in the doorway, triumphantly surveying the havoc. "I knew he'd miss me!"

I stood speechless, still clutching Matt's arm while she flipped her chair rightside up, replaced the cushions, rummaged through the mess for an ashtray and plopped herself down amid the debris.

"Actually," she leaned forward, "when I heard the commotion I hadda come back up. I know you been wantin' t' see my son without me. But you can see for yourself the kid ain't ready."

Chapter 6

"THE reason I'm callin', see—" She sounded panicked. "Frankie—Frankie's plant had a breakdown. He's home an' he wants t' bring Matt t' see you. He says he's payin' for my time, he's got a right t' use it. I tole him Miss Craig can't change 'pointments like that."

"Your time is for you," I agreed, "unless," I suggested it cautiously, "you'd like to come together. The whole family."

"I'll tell him he hasta bring my son back . . ." her voice tapered off.

Frank Barringer was pale, his eyes wild. Gone the earlier cockiness. Matt walked by himself, guided by his father's clenched hand on the collar of his shirt. Mr. Barringer maneuvered his son like a puppet—up the stairs, into the office. When he let go, the boy collapsed in front of the chair his mother always occupied, resting his head on the seat, and cried softly.

His father paced around the room and lit a cigarette with trembling hands. "That kid," he yelled. "That kid! Nearly killed us both. Reached right over and switched off the ignition key. Can you believe that? While we was on the turnpike? Oh my God!" He covered his eyes, then wiped his hands down his face. "Trucks, buses, everything swervin' not t' ram us. Power steering—the whole works was off, while I'm fightin' the kid t' get the keys outta his hands.

"Then—then," he shouted, "I finally got the truck goin' an' he starts kickin' out the windshield. Thought the glass was gonna go." He glowered down at the cowering child, who'd begun rocking on his back, his arms covering his ears and eyes.

"Look, ya gotta help me." Mr. Barringer finally sat down. A little color was returning to his face, but his eyes were creased in lines of strain. "Whatever he does, he's my kid. He's my boy. My son." His voice cracked. "I wantcha to help me with him now, 'cause I think he needs a man. Someday he won't need me when everything's goin' smooth. Right now I'll take care of him. But you gotta help me straighten him out.

"His mother, she won't listen. I dunno what she tole you goes on at that house, how he shits all over the furniture and don't mind no one." His voice tightened with anger. "Now he got a new trick. I sit down to supper, see. I like my meal served soon as I get home. So I'm eatin' an' he runs in and spits in my eyes. What does she do? She laughs. Sometimes I think it's her that's nuts."

The boy stopped rocking and lay motionless.

Hands shaking, his father lit another cigarette. "I dunno. There's a lot of crazies in her family, but Nellie didn't grow up with them. Me—" he jabbed at his chest—"I think she's still scared of something happened years ago. She says she don't remember, but she usta cry about it all the time." He took a long drag on the cigarette.

"It was her brother, not Calvin, see, not her real brother. The son of the woman who ran the foster home. He tells her her girlfriend's waitin' in some garage. So she goes over there like he says. Only it's really all his buddies, a whole gang. Makes me sick what they done t' her." He paused, clutching his stomach. "She was only eleven," his voice choked. "They was all eighteen. Nineteen.

"Crazy thing," he said very slowly, "it was Nellie who felt like she done somethin' wrong. She never told on them guys because she felt so dirty. I'd like to meet them just two minutes. Just two minutes with each one of those bastards."

He sat in silence for several moments, clenching his fists fitfully. "That's why she thinks somethin' bad's gonna happen to Matt. She don't trust nobody. That's why she's so overprotective."

The boy jumped up, grabbed both his father's hands and tried to pull him out of the chair.

"No, son," the man spoke patiently. "I ain't leavin' yet."

The boy tugged harder, straining, screaming, grunting, but his father didn't budge.

"Not til I'm done talkin' ta' Miss Craig." He looked at me. "You got some paper an' crayons?" I handed him both, with the warning that Matt had chewed the crayons before.

"These ain't for eatin', see!" He shook the box in the boy's face. "Now sit down and color till I'm through." Matt dropped to the floor in front of his father—the first time I'd seen him obey. Dumping out all the crayons, he began to scribble with three at once, red, green and yellow squiggles on the manila paper.

"I still think the kid hurt his brain," his father pointed to his head, "banging his head all the time. Even as a baby he had his 'tizzies'—what Nellie calls them. I usta wake up hearin' the baby smashing his head on the crib. She never thought nothin' was wrong. But me—I always did."

"I think the head-banging is a symptom more than a cause," I said. "I wish we did know just what's wrong. You know, I'm beginning to think we can't help Matt enough with just one hour a week."

He gave me a puzzled look.

"I haven't talked to anyone about this, in fact

I'm really thinking out loud, but maybe the Society for Aid to the Retarded could provide a program for Matt five days a week this summer. We can't do that here and it's what he really needs—a daily program."

Eyes narrowed, he'd stopped smoking to listen intently. "Well," he began, clearing his throat, "wouldn't that leave her all alone too much?" So that was his first concern.

"They'd let her stay, too, in the beginning."

"That's what I'm here for, see." His confidence returning, he blew a series of smoke rings which wafted upward. "So you an' me can make a plan. I'm not gonna let her keep that kid as her defense against the world. Hey!" He darted out of the chair. "Get them outta your mouth!"

Matt's cheeks ballooned out with crayons. His father reached for him angrily and, taking Matt's head, shook it until the boy spat the multi-colored glob onto the floor.

"Pick up every damn piece!" His face mottled with rage, Mr. Barringer prodded his son with the toe of his boot. Matt sat motionless.

"Now!" he nudged him harder. "Right now!" The boy didn't move.

"You son of a gun!" his father's teeth were clenched. Grabbing the boy's hands in his, he forced him to pick up the wet wax ball of half-eaten crayons.

"Now drop it in the basket!" Mr. Barringer

rapped the boy's hand against the top of the waste-basket. "Let go! You stubborn little bastard! Let go!"

Matt glared at his father defiantly, then slowly uncupped his hand, dropping the soggy mess into the container. Mr. Barringer released him and turned away to the window, muttering to himself. "Spoiled little bastard . . ."

The boy started screeching. But it was a different sound, like the "caw" of a blue jay. "Gw-aa! Gw-aa!" He put his hands on his father's back and tried to turn him toward the door. "Gw-aa! Gw-aa!" It sounded as though Matt was trying to speak.

He stepped back across the room, then ran at his father, ramming the top of his head into the man's lower back. "Gw-aaa! Gw-aaa!"

"Mr. Barringer—those sounds Matt's making!" I could hardly contain my excitement. "I think he's saying "go on! go on!""

"Naw." Caught off balance, Matt's last shove pushed him several feet ahead. "That's his noise when he wants me out." He spoke over his shoulder as they were leaving. "He makes it every morning."

A sound to indicate a desire in a given situation—that had to be called speech. And now I knew this child had at least a minimal ability to communicate. I had to curb an impulse of wild hope. I'm not sure how many times the intercom buzzed before I heard it.

"Mrs. Barringer on line two," Sylvia said. "She's called every ten minutes while they were in with you."

I pushed the second button. Her jarring voice roared out. "Hey Craigie! See, the reason I called, see, I called t' tell ye I got rid of that stinkin' dog. Police just took it away. I says I dunno whose it is—must be a stray. Frankie's gonna be mad I called them." No remorse—a hint of glee—Frankie's punishment for taking her appointment. ". . . But it ain't Frankie who's scared a that stinkin' animal. Now—" Her tone became wheedling. "What was you two talkin' about, huh? What'd you two say about me?"

"Why didn't you come with them? I missed you!"

"Lissen, I'm really lonesome without that kid. Awful lonesome. But it's good for him, ain't it? Bein' with a man?"

"That's right. It is good for him. And they'll both be home soon. You'll have them both home till the plant equipment's fixed."

"You think that's good? Lookin' at Frankie's stinkin' puss till Monday? Ha! I like it better when he's gone. I'll be glad when they finish rewirin' the laundry and he goes back t' work. I'm more alone when I'm with him."

"You're pretty angry that he brought Matt in . . ."

"Ever since he got that classy job, fixin' them machines, he treats me like one a his workers.

'Manager' they call him—big fancy deal! Seems like he picks a argument now just to be the winner." Then she drawled her words seductively. "So tell me 'bout your stinkin' little meeting."

"We talked about a new idea, Mrs. Barringer. It might be really great for Matt. A program five days a week all summer. Awhile ago I wouldn't have suggested it. But now I think he's ready. We won't make any plans until you meet the person who runs it. She could tell us all the details. But having him learning every day would . . ."

"Lissen! Frankie ain't got no right talkin' about programs for my son!" Suddenly she was screaming hysterically. "It's not even Frankie's kid! He's not his father!"

I was shocked. "Not his father?" I echoed.

"Matt's real father's dead! Lissen—" She breathed deeply. "Louie drove a tractor for the town, see. An'—an' the whole thing turned over down the dump. Broke his neck on top of all that garbage. Matt was only three, see," she'd begun to sniff, struggling to maintain control, "so—so Frankie ain't his real father at all."

(I could still hear Mr. Barringer's voice. "He's my son. My boy.")

"It wasn't no marriage anyhow." She was calmer now. "I never let him near me after work. That bum never washed, so he always smelled like that garbage. An' afterwards I wanted t' sue the town, see, for more confensation—more money for Matt's sake.

"But then I met Frankie. He was workin' for the laundry, pickin' up clothes for the woman ran the boardin' house where me an' Matt was livin'. An' Frankie says we don't want confensation. He's too proud, see. Says we don't need the money.

"He says soon as Matt's better we're gonna take him on a boat to Europe. Still . . ." She sounded wistful. "Sometimes I blame Frankie. I coulda had more than what I do."

I was still stunned, grappling with the words I'd just heard him say. "I usta wake up hearing the baby smashing his head on the crib," he'd told me. How could that be if the real father hadn't died until the child was three?

"I s'pose he tole ya my son spits at him."

"That's one of the things you and I can change."

"Not me! I'd get a headache tryin'. So when's this meetin' 'bout the summer? Does she know he can't leave me? Ooops. Here comes Frankie. Gotta go tell him his dog's gone."

Chapter 7

FLORENCE Hunter, head of the private agency, Aid to the Retarded, sounded dubious about trying Matt in one of the small play groups they ran in the summer. "These children are gentle," she said. "From what you say, this boy would terrify them."

I tried to explain the pressures I felt. Every day wasted at home widened the gap between Matt and other children. He, more than most, needed mental stimulation daily, not just one hour a week. No place within commuting distance except their agency would know how to deal with him.

Teachers, not psychologists or therapists, had most to offer this boy. If nothing more than separating him from his mother could be accomplished over the summer, the Planning and Placement Team from the public school would then be able to consider his needs when they met in September.

I knew the team might decide there was no plan, no program in the city for a child like Matt. But then Ceil Black would look into private schools, residential treatment centers and state institutions. The city would pay for a program elsewhere if these places had none to offer.

Florence listened noncommittally.

She called back later. "We have an extra teacher in our infant program. She's been working with babies who've been identified as high risk for developmental difficulties. She's willing to see your boy one or two hours a day. I think she'd be good with him."

Florence and the teacher agreed to meet the Barringers at the Center. If they were willing to accept Matt, we'd know that very day.

Mrs. Barringer and I discussed their coming. I wrote down the list of questions she wanted to ask. She was reasonably calm until they arrived. Then she lapsed into painful, silent self-consciousness, rarely lifting her eyes to look at me and never turning in their direction.

And Matt was frightened too. His back to the two strange people, he never left his mother's lap.

Florence and the teacher took turns explaining how they help children understand new concepts, begin to socialize, perhaps even to speak. Finally they asked if she had any questions.

"Miss Craig," Mrs. Barringer pleaded in a husky whisper, "you tell them." While I read the questions we'd prepared, she sat rocking her crying boy.

Florence was reassuring. "Yes, mothers may stay at first. Miss Kelly here could transport you both . . . The cost is twenty dollars weekly." And then she said, responding to Mrs. Barringer's gasp, "We are well endowed so that we can adjust the fee for every child."

"It ain't that we don't got plenty a money," Mrs. Barringer said slowly, without looking up. "Fact is, we're gonna fix that house up pretty soon. We ordered that kinda linoleum rug that got colored designs like pieces of yarn. You know, it looks just like a carpet. Frankie says it's three-forty-nine a runnin' foot, but he didn't even run. Just walked around t' measure the floor.

"But Frankie won it, see, playin' them numbers last week. I tole him t' stop givin' that man so much money, but finally he won. A hunnert bucks! When he showed me first, I thought it was phony. But he says, 'Hold it, it's real.'"

Florence glanced at me. We both smiled.

"But, ya see—" Mrs. Barringer looked up timidly. "He don't always win, ya see. An' then— then we ain't got enough."

"I understand." Florence nodded. "Do you think you could pay ten dollars a week?"

"I'll ask Frankie." Nellie was facing Florence more directly. "Then when he wins at them numbers, we could pay more those weeks.

"Ya know, me an' Frankie is really glad about your program. 'Cause from what you say, what youse people do makes a lot more sense than anybody else." Her eyes darted in my direction. "It's like a—a better environment!" she said enthusiastically. "In a way Miss Craig, here, had some pretty good ideas. Like takin' him to the bathroom at home. But her ideas don't work sometimes. Some kids just ain't ready."

I couldn't believe it. She was flattering the two strangers she'd been so frightened of, courting them at my expense.

"An' another thing I tole Frankie—" Once she had started she just wouldn't stop. "My son's smarter than Miss Craig when it comes t' doin' puzzles. I noticed that myself. An' Frankie says it ain't right, for a kid t' be smarter than the teacher."

The young teacher stared at Florence, who lowered her head to conceal a grin.

"So—hey! What're ya doin' that for?" Matt began drumming his fists on her shoulders, lightly at first, harder with each blow.

"Cut it out." She tried to catch his hands.

He slipped from her lap and stood in front of her. Looking around in panic, sobbing tearlessly, he tried to pull her up.

"G-waaa." He jumped a tantrum dance. "G-waaa!"

That wonderful sound again. No doubt about it. He meant "go on."

"My son wants t' go now." She sighed as she rose. "So which one a you is pickin' us up?"

They'll never accept him now, I thought. But Nancy Kelly wrote something and handed it to her. "To remind you. I'll be at your house July fifth at nine."

With an air of accomplishment, head held high, Mrs. Barringer took her son's hand. For the first time, she walked him down the stairs. His whimpering grew fainter, then disappeared altogether as the outside door banged shut.

"That's great!" I clapped Nancy's shoulder. "But how come you agreed? He was awfully . . ."

"You're right." She nodded seriously, then turned to wink at Florence. "But we had to get the kid a smarter teacher. Now I, myself, always got A on puzzles."

"Of course Mrs. Barringer resents you," Leora said later. "After all, you've tried to help her child. She'll denigrate anyone who attempts to do that."

Some of my best thinking occurs when I'm cleaning up—myself, the floor, kitchen counters. That night, bent over the sink to shampoo my hair, I suddenly realized that Matt had become upset at exactly ten-thirty-five.

It was precisely that time just the week

before when he'd discovered she'd left the room. I knew definitely. When he'd thrown everything off my desk, the clock had stopped at ten-thirty-five.

Could he have made that connection today by seeing a clock? Or was he mysteriously warned by some inner alarm that something frightening might happen unless they left quickly?

Chapter 8

THE last few sessions with the Barringers, before the summer program, aroused in me a sense of urgency. You're not helpless, I wanted her to know. You can do something about Matt's problems, if you're willing to work for the changes you want.

But she had a message of her own. I doubt she listened to mine. "Be sure that teacher knows my son's got a handicap," she'd say with rising apprehension. "*You* know how handicapped people think. But what if *she* don't understand?"

Matt himself delighted me. He'd begun to lead the way from waiting room to the office. I'd walk behind them, routinely counting every step.

He'd dash into the room as if he'd waited all week
to get there.

His flight into health, I wanted to believe.
And his play changed, too. Crouched on the floor,
he'd learned to spin the top, to construct tall towers
of blocks. Not much, perhaps, from a six-year-old,
but it was progress, compared with the earlier
sessions. He often made brief visits to his mother's
side now, watching her face intently as she spoke.
But he no longer climbed on her lap.

Frankie, too, apparently saw a difference.
"He says Matt's improvin' so much he took him
down the laundry t' pick up his check. An' while
they was there, Matt met Carlton, Frankie's friend.
A colored man. Frankie was real proud cause Matt
didn't hardly cry at all. Carlton coulda took it
personal, ya know, cause Frankie says they're real
sensitive, them people."

I wondered if Matt was better because she
hadn't been there, communicating her own fears.
But in spite of the progress, she continued to tell the
depressing stories of her family. "Gloria's gotta see
the judge. She an' some bum had a fight right out in
the street. She thinks the state is gonna take her
kids.

"My brother's got arrested again. Stealin'
them suitcases down the airport.

"The other brother set a fire to the place his
wife's shackin' up. Just did it outta spite. But he's
back now in the loony bin."

We started our last hour talking about the

new program, her getting Matt ready daily, their being driven by Miss Kelly.

"Me an' Frankie ordered eighteen pairs a pants for Matt, an' twenty-one new shirts. We want him lookin' nice." In the last few minutes her bravado faded. "I'm really scared, Miss Craig." Her lips trembled.

"That's understandable," I nodded, "feeling scared about something new. But you'll be fine. I know because of all the other new things you've done recently."

"Mmm." She looked dubious. "But I'm still more scared than other people. Counta what Frankie says he tole ya happened t' me one time.

"Ya know what I mean—" She began to recite it haltingly, a horror story of rape and abuse by older boys when she was eleven years old.

Repeating it, I hoped, would enable her to feel some mastery over what had been a terrifying experience. Yet I knew it would have been better if she'd had help in dealing with her feelings long ago, when it happened. Rape, like accidents, divorce and death, is a psychological emergency best dealt with as quickly as possible. Left alone, the emotional scars become deep rooted, more burdensome, yet ever more obscure. When she finished talking, we sat in silence. Tears coursed down her face and onto her blouse.

I struggled to keep my own voice steady. "No—no wonder you're so frightened." I put my hand on her arm. "You've had some pretty bad times."

"Jeez," she gasped, blotting tears with her sleeve. "You can say that again."

When it was time to say goodbye, I finally realized how involved I'd become with this pair. I would miss them. And there was a chance, I wanted to believe, that Matt would improve dramatically. Despite his limitations, there were those tantalizing flashes of intelligence. I couldn't help wishing that I were the teacher who was about to see him daily.

We were going downstairs when I heard what sounded like a command. Matt was several steps ahead.

"Wun!" someone shouted.

Though no one else was around, I couldn't believe it was he.

"Doo!" he moved down a step.

"Dree!" another step.

"Pour!" He was on the landing.

"Matt! Matt! You're counting!" I was astounded. "That's wonderful!" I caught him in my arms and swept him high. "One, two, three, four! That's right! Good for you!" Mouth ajar—blue eyes vacant—no smile—no joy—no response.

"Mrs. Barringer." I swung around, still holding Matt. "Wasn't that great? To hear Matt count?" She hesitated, backing a few steps away, leery, uncertain. Any pleasure from Matt earning such praise was lost, I knew then, in seeing him in my arms. I put him down quickly.

"Should I tell Frankie," her voice was cool, restrained, "my son was good t'day?"

Early summer brought a stream of agitated parents to the counselling center, shepherding apathetic youngsters who'd failed the year in school. We'd begin each case with a history of the family, its past and recent problems. While causes and possible remedies were being explored, there were immediate plans to consider: tutoring, summer classes, a private school, repeating the grade, a drug-treatment program.

I had to find a summer camp for two boys who'd worn out their welcomes in foster homes every vacation. Then there were records to update, state reports to file, court appearance in a custody fight. And always a summer tragedy: I was assigned to work with the parents and sisters of a girl who'd drowned on a Sunday outing.

Nancy Kelly called in mid-July to ask me to take Mrs. Barringer out so she could see Matt alone. He'd been impossibly wild the whole first week, and dangerous in her car. "Even in his mother's arms, I thought he'd kick out the windshield," she said. "In fact, my dashboard and glove compartment are pretty well dented." Over the weekend she'd decided to quit. Neither she nor the car could take his abuse. But on Monday he'd been strangely calm.

"I really think he'd expected to see me Saturday and Sunday and decided I didn't come

because of his behavior. I could see he was, well—
almost pleased when I picked them up, and later
that day he tried to shove his mother out of the
room. She may not be ready, but I'd like to see him
alone."

For a while I sat beside Mrs. Barringer in the
back of the room, watching Nancy work with Matt.
Wisely, she'd kept the room barren, no distracting
toys or pictures. One at a time, she'd withdraw an
item from the metal cabinet to her right and try to
interest Matt.

She sat cross-legged on the floor. He was
lying on his side. She showed him a stacking toy
and then a pegboard. He'd watch the new item a
moment, then roll away, making whining, puppy-
dog whimpers. She had to get up and chase him to
retrieve some pegs from his mouth.

"No, no," she chided, holding the back of
his head to keep him still while she probed for the
pegs. When she'd gotten all five, he sat up and spat
directly on her cheek.

"No spitting!" She didn't stop to wipe the
dribble. "You look at me!" She cupped his chin in
her hands. "No spitting." He refused to look at her
face, rolling his eyes both left and right, skipping
over Nancy as though she didn't exist. Then he
caught a glimpse of me, sitting by his mother. I
wondered if he'd remember.

He got up slowly, his gaze fixed on my hair,
carefully avoiding contact with my eyes. Turning
his head to keep me in view, he walked all around

the room—letting his right hand glide along each wall as a blind person might. The second time around he moved in closer—a yard or so. He walked around us five or six times, each orbit veering nearer to our chairs. Finally, he was so close I could have touched him. His mother sat rigidly, staring ahead as though she were afraid of what might happen.

"Hi, Matt." I said softly. "I'm really glad to see you." Agitated, he jumped back, and began circling faster.

"Wun?" It was a question. He kept walking. "WUN?" he shouted frantically. "Doo?" He began yanking at his hair. "DOO?"

"That's right, Matt. One, two. You counted with me. You're doing it again. One—two." So this was to be our greeting, our signal of recognition.

Satisfied, he ran back to Nancy, and rolled on the floor in front of her like an animal seeking gratification. It seemed like a good time to leave.

"Mother and I are going out. We'll be back very soon," I said.

Nancy said goodbye as she patted Matt. "You little monkey. You didn't let on you could count!"

"Mm—mm—mm," he was making a happy sound although his face was blank. He didn't look back.

Mrs. Barringer moved stiffly out to the hall and refused to go any further. "My son may need me," she insisted. I stood whispering to her, outside the door, about how well he was doing, while I waited to hear him scream. But he didn't. It was she, now, who needed him. "What if he gets hurt or somethin'?" Within fifteen minutes she was so agitated we had to return to the room.

The Society for Aid to the Retarded rented basement rooms in an old stone church. On Tuesday Mrs. Barringer and I got as far as the concrete stairs outside, and sat talking, facing the tidy cemetery.

"You think it's right," she bit down on her thumbnail, "leaving Matt alone with that girl?"

I assured her I did.

"Well I feel sorta funny," she chewed on another nail, "leavin' them by theirselves. She's pretty young I mean, t' really be a teacher. An' a lotta times when I'm watchin' her I feel like sayin' all right you two, now break it up."

"I guess you feel left out . . ."

"A person would be crazy not ta! That teacher is maybe smart in some things. Like she says my son does all that cryin' cause he wants his own way. Now, I buy that. But her skirts is just too high."

Even hearing about her family was a relief from her concern for Matt. I managed to get her to talk about them for awhile.

"Gloria says she's gonna send me some clothes my brother got in them suitcases—the ones he took at the airport 'fore he got caught. But I dunno about Frankie. He's gonna ast me where they come from. An' he's gettin' awful bossy now. Thinks I don't know nothin'. He never even ordered the makeup I chose in the book. I kept waitin' to get it—Matt's clothes came, but not the stuff I wanted.

"So Frankie says I'd look like a clown, paintin' stuff on my face. Honest, Miss Craig, I was so disappointed. I oughta decide what I wanna wear. I think a woman gotta have rights, too."

The sun felt good on my face and body. I was enjoying sitting outside, talking to her. Maybe 'women's lib' was a good approach. I'd tell her that others, like herself, once felt a lack of confidence and found a way to change.

"You know," I began, "that's what a lot of women are thinking now. About their rights . . ."

"Yeah? I think I heard it on TV. So in other words, if a woman wants t' wear makeup she oughta be able t' do it?"

"Well, that's what women are talking about—deciding things for themselves. About their lives, their bodies, equal pay and equal opportunity."

"Now I think that part's disgustin'!" She was momentarily angry. "Takin' opportunity of someone else." Then a mental leap: "Like that girl in the room with my son. Maybe I shouldn't look at her in the sense of a woman. But I hope my son don't take no opportunity."

Wednesday, too, we sat on the steps. Again she complained about leaving Matt, before chang-
·ing the subject.

"I bin thinkin'," she was pulling threads from the hem of her pink cotton dress, "like about them other women you tole me, havin' opinions I mean.

"Last night I was lookin' at Frankie, watchin' TV like a zombie. I ast him t' talk t' me, but not about that stinkin' laundry. I think he got mad just so he could watch TV. But he says there's no sense us talkin', the way I'm treatin' Matt. Then he says my son's bein' retarded is all my fault, 'cause of the way I baby him. Honest, Miss Craig, that makes me feel awful bad."

This time I offered no comfort. Her anxiety, I hoped, would prod her to change.

It was another beautiful summer day, the sun bright, the breeze gentle. "Remember them clothes Gloria promised t' send me?" She plucked at the grass by the stairs where we sat. "Well first I hadda send her ten bucks for the mailin' is what she said. But when the box come, I seen by them stamps it only cost a dollar. An' none a them stinkin' things fit. Three lousy skirts, I couldn't even get one a them on.

"So I calls her for my ten bucks an' her rotten boyfriend hangs right up in my face. I dialed him right back. I says, 'Lissen punk, you do that again, I'll spit in your eye.'

"Then Gloria gets on. She says she'll crack him over the head with the phone. You know—not the part you talk into, but the part you dial. Then she says she can't return the money 'cause she's helpin' my brother pay the lawyer for when he goes t' court—for stealin' them things." She chewed thoughtfully on a long blade of grass.

Today, I was discouraged and annoyed with her stories. Whether or not it was intentional, the tales enabled her to avoid more meaningful talk. I'd been hoping she would take the initiative in bringing up Matt's paternity again, but I'd grown impatient waiting for this to happen. It was over a month ago that she'd told me Frankie wasn't Matt's real father. And she'd been angry at him at the time. Perhaps it wasn't even true. I decided to confront her.

"I've been thinking about the time you called me when your husband brought in Matt. You told me something then you haven't mentioned since. I've been wondering why."

"About Matt's not Frankie's kid?" She knew right away what I meant.

"Mmmm."

"Remember I tole you I was married before, an' Louie had a accident?"

"So Matt's real father's dead."

"Broke his neck in that garbage dump."

"I'm sorry." We sat in silence on the steps of the church. Then she checked her pockets, found and lit a cigarette.

"I ain't gonna lie t' you, Miss Craig." She exhaled a stream of smoke. "Matt ain't Louie's kid either. Like I say, it was no kinda marriage. See, it's pretty hard t' tell ya how it was . . . Sometimes I was bad, see . . ." I waited but she'd lowered her head onto her arms. I couldn't tell if she was crying.

"You've had a hard life," I prodded softly. "I think you did the best you could."

"No, no," she shook her head, without looking up. "I was real, real bad. I mean," she sniffed, "sometimes I didn't even know the guys that usta come an' visit while Louie went t' work . . ." Her voice was barely audible. ". . . an' that's when—when I got Matt." She sounded anguished. "I don't even know his father, see." She was still bent over.

"You were brave to tell me." I was stunned by this new perspective on her life. "I know it's hard to talk about."

"When Frankie starts comin' to the boardin' house—he was workin' for a different laundry then—he always says he'd like t' see the baby. I didn't give him no laundry t' clean at all, but he kept showin' up an' talkin' t' me. An' he never ast for nothin', like them other guys. An' that's how we got started.

"After Louie's accident, Frankie says we're gettin' married, see. I tole him he gotta be kiddin'. But he says I'm startin' life again, an' he's takin' care of me an' my son. So that's the truth, see. That's what happened."

I thanked her for sharing her painful memories.

"What I guess ya' oughta know, Miss Craig, is me an' Frankie is tryin' t' live a decent life."

"I do know that."

We looked at each other and smiled.

"Let's go out for a ride," I said the following day. She agreed right away. We said goodbye to Nancy and Matt and, for the first time, she left her son in someone else's care.

She was, I felt immediately, more at ease with me. Dressed casually, in yellow slacks and a white sleeveless blouse, her auburn hair caught in a long single braid, she looked younger and more relaxed than ever. She curled up in the front seat of the car, her legs tucked under her body, and talked as we headed downtown.

"You woulda laughed at me an' Frankie last night." She slapped her ample thigh. "We was such hot stuff. I started tellin' him I felt bad about not gettin' that makeup, see, and guess what Frankie says? 'You win,' he says. 'So go ahead an' order it again.'

"I could see he was in such a swell mood I decided t' ast him, how 'bout paintin' the kitchen? Honest, Miss Craig, them walls is so filthy. Then what d' ya' think he says?" This time she waited.

"I give up."

"'Ooooh no!'" She mimicked his emphatic response. "'Youse women,' Frankie says, 'you wanta try an' be like men? So go ahead an' do it! You can paint the kitchen yourself.'"

"What did you say to that?" I figured that she'd be angry.

"I says t' bring me home a lotta paint. Pink oughta look nice. But we was talkin' so good I even ast him somethin' else. See, I wanted him t' buy a 'cyclopedia for Matt. For my son's welfare, I mean. But Frankie says by the time Matt can read, they'll be writin' new stuff in them books. Frankie's real smart about business." She shrugged. "I hadda agree."

A Volkswagen to my right was pulling out. On impulse I decided to take the parking space, to be within walking distance of a discount store. While I parked the car she kept talking, unaware of my plan to take her shopping.

"This morning Frankie was still jokin' about me wantin' so much. Know what he says? He's right in a way. Frankie says I been gettin' pretty pushy ever since I been talkin' t' you."

I laughed. "Then push your way out of the car. You and I are going shopping."

"In that big store there. Uh-uh!" She extended both hands as though signaling stop. "I never been in a apartment store. No, honest, Miss Craig, I'll go some other day. What if my son's cryin' for me? We been gone too long. We oughta get back right now."

"Matt's doing fine, you know that." I

reached over her to open the door to her right. "Besides, it's time you and I had a little fun. C'mon. Push over. I'm getting out your side, too."

Reluctantly, she let me ease her out of the car.

"Let's go!" I had to pull her into the store, while she protested: "I never seen a place needin' so many doors. Makes my head ache. How d'ya know which one t' go in? This place is too confusin'."

She was right. It was a confusing store. She stood at the front, her mouth open, an expression of childlike wonder in her rounded eyes, while I tried to figure the way to Women's Wear.

"Ain't that disgustin'!" She whispered hoarsely, pointing to underwear on display. "Puttin' stuff like that where anyone can see it!"

Then she began lingering over the blouses and sweaters, feeling the materials. "Ain't this one pretty? Hey, I really like that purple color. But who'd wear a shirt like that? Them shirts is just for freaks."

She toyed with all the jewelry strewn in plastic trays on a glassed-in display of watches. "Hey, this is a pin. This little cat. Ain't that cute, he's got diamonds for eyes. Wow, look at that frog made outta gold. My mother usta tell us never touch them filthy things—real frogs, I mean."

By this time three giggling sales girls had clustered to watch us an aisle away. They moved as we did throughout the store, punctuating her monologue with spasms of stifled laughter. But she didn't seem to notice.

Fall and winter coats were already on display. "Remember you said you needed one?"

She scraped a few hangers along the steel rack, disparaging each coat she touched. "Ain't that ugly!" she roared. "These coats is all for old ladies." Suddenly she looked at me as if she were frightened. "Ooops!" She slapped her hand on her mouth. "No offense intended."

"Hey." I put my hands on my hips. "Thanks a lot!"

"No really, Miss Craig. What I mean is they'd look better on you. Why don't ya try one on? Can ya do that without payin'?" She looked around guardedly. "How d' ya know how much they go for?" The sales girls turned away, shaking their heads and pointing in our direction.

"Each ticket tells. See, twenty-seven dollars."

"Twenty-seven dollars! Man, they're crazy. I seen mink coats in one of them catalogues for twenty-five bucks. Let's get outta here." We walked empty-handed through the speed checkout.

"Hey wait." She stopped by the television magazines on sale by the cash register.

"Gee," she said wistfully, bending to squint at the cover picture of the Waltons. "That's what I wish my family was like. Them people on TV. I seen that show. They all act so nice to each other.

Yup, I wish my family was more like them Waltons."

"Television stories don't show real people under real pressure . . ."

"Do we hafta go back already?" she interrupted.

"No, Nancy has Matt another hour. Is there something else you'd like to do?"

"Oh, I dunno." Suddenly her enthusiasm was gone. Back out in the summer heat she slumped into the car listlessly and smoked in silence while I maneuvered out of the cramped parking space.

Turning away from me, she stared out the side window. "I guess I feel like stayin' out." Just a half hour ago she'd been anxious to get back to Matt.

"Funny—" she mused bitterly, "funny that teacher waited til you an' me was out on them steps before she give my son them crackers. I could tell anyway. He had crumbs all down his front when we got back." When she spoke again her voice was small. "Nobody's givin' me any treats."

"I'm pretty hungry right now." I felt like an actor responding to his cue. "Want to go to Howard Johnson's?"

"That stuck-up orange place?" She ground her cigarette into the floor mat with the sole of her shoe. "Uh-uh! You'd never get me in there."

"Hmmm . . ." I tried to think of someplace close by.

"Turn here!" She pointed right. "Keep goin'
straight, t' that diner over by my house. Frankie
says the food's real good."

The only other customers at Home Diner
were three men in spattered carpenter pants, tee
shirts and painters' caps, drinking coffee at the
counter. There were six maroon booths, each
mended with strips of bright red tape. Mrs. Barringer slid into the second one and drummed her
fingers impatiently until the waiter arrived with
menus.

"I don't need one a them. I know what I'm
havin'. I'm havin' split pea soup, minute steak,
french fries an' some a them baked beans. That's
what Frankie orders here."

I decided that I'd better eat lunch, too, but
even a sandwich was hard to face at eleven.

"Hey whatcha got there?" She plopped
down the soup bowl she'd been drinking from, to
grab the top slice of bread off my plate. "Jeez! Don't
eat that!" She probed my roast beef sandwich with
her finger. "It ain't even cooked."

"I like it rare." I slapped the bread in place
and took a big bite, hoping she'd eat and keep quiet.

"Meat like that," she slurped a spoonful of
soup, "is gonna give you worms." I felt my stomach turn.

She ate her french fries, coated in catsup.
"So ·what ya gonna make for supper, huh?" I
thought if I talked about meatless meals it might
keep her mind off my roast beef.

"Oh, I don't know. Clam chowder, maybe, or tuna . . ."

"Know what?" Grinning, she elbowed me across the table. "You must be real dumb when it comes t' cookin'."

"What makes you think so?" I decided to forget the sandwich.

" 'Cause women goin' out t' work don't care nothin' about makin' food. I bet you don't never peel potatoes. I bet—" she stabbed the air with a french fry, "I bet," giggling now, she was having trouble finishing the sentence, "you can't—boil—water."

"No fair! I'm a good cook. Lots of women who work . . ."

"You probably—" she enjoyed herself more with each indictment, "you probably cook TV dinners." Our waiter, wiping glasses behind the counter, looked over and chuckled.

"What's that creep grinnin' at?" She waved at him, moving one finger at a time and smiling flirtatiously.

I began to feel as giddy as she, although for different reasons. My husband often teased me about my work. "How come," he liked to say, "you waste your time with the people I've spent my life avoiding?" I tried to imagine his comments if he'd heard the conversation here.

After we finished, we had trouble trying to cross the boulevard to my car. Mrs. Barringer dashed back to the sidewalk every time a truck appeared. Finally I grabbed her hand. We scurried through the traffic like two capricious schoolgirls, then leaned against the hood of the car panting and laughing.

"I'm tellin' Frankie you almost got us killed."

"Then I'm telling Frankie you flirted with the waiter." She giggled. We held our faces up to the warmth of the sun.

"You're gettin' pretty familiar, callin' my husband his first name." I felt her elbow dig into my ribs. "No, honest though, Miss Craig, why don't ya call me Nellie? It'd seem more like we're friends, know what I mean?"

"Sure. And will you call me Eleanor?"

"Uh-uh! Craigie's easier." Cars zoomed by while we rested in easy silence.

"I dunno why," she closed her eyes, "but somehow I feel kinda different inside." Her eyes stayed shut. "I dunno why," she said more slowly, "but—somehow—I feel a new kind of happy."

Chapter 9

THE week after those daily meetings with Nellie, Nancy began picking up Matt alone. Although his mother had agreed on this procedure, she phoned me five times the first day Matt left her. When I objected to the interruption, she started calling just before the hour, when my appointments changed, realizing that I was more apt to be free.

"The reason I'm callin', see—that teacher just picked Matt up. He went in her car real good. But she says I oughta go out myself and I ain't got nowhere t' go."

"The reason I'm callin' see, I'm tryin' t' paint the kitchen. But they gave Frankie the wrong color—red insteada pink."

". . . I just found out, my sister's husband's back. Got a good job too, cleanin' up in a nursin' home. But Gloria says he's stealin' off the guy who runs the place."

". . . I was just sittin' here watchin' that 'mergency pattern on TV. It's awful borin'. Know what I mean?"

I finally limited her to one call a day. But this was hard to enforce. Nellie became more and more manipulative.

"How come Craigie can't talk right now?" she'd demand of the secretary. "I got a special problem, see. Who's she got in that office t'day?"

At the end of the week I called to make an appointment with her and told her she'd have to save her problems until we met. I hoped my being less available would force her to face the reality that Matt would be gone and she'd have to find new interests—perhaps even a friend. When I finally saw her, she rushed in talking about a neighbor and I thought the strategy had worked.

"Ya know that woman lives right down the street, couple a houses before ya get t' mine?" Nellie paced back and forth as she ranted. "Well, soon as Matt's teacher come t' pick him up t'day, she yells down the road an' asts me in for coffee."

At last she sat down, and groped in her purse until she found the cigarettes. "Well, I never walked down that road before, 'cause a them dogs—me bein' scared a them an' all. But I did it, I went t' her house, an' everythin' looked so nice inside. An'—an' we sat in the kitchen t'gether, just like human bein's, an' I was feelin' real happy," she smiled, "thinkin' how enjoyable I felt. But," she shook her head sadly, "I'll never think that again.

"I didn't know she wanted me there just for her c'venience." Nellie's voice faded as she turned from me to look out the window. "But then she tells me what's on her mind. She seen my son jump on the roof of her car while we was waitin' for his ride.

"So I says, 'My, aren't we touchy! My son got on it accidently, 'cause his teacher was late. An' when he gets mad he tries t' punish other people. But that's 'cause he don't understand, so I don't let nobody pick at him.'

"An' then I says, 'Lissen, I seen your car, an' your car's a piece a shit. An' I seen your kid out the window, an' he needs help almost as much as mine. Only we don't bury our heads in the sand. We get him what he needs, includin' that umbrella shot they advertise on TV.'

"Well, that hussy almost took my head off. We both kept screamin' at each other. I was yellin' that the reason I don't have no fancy furniture like her is 'cause my son would wreck it up right now. So her stinkin' car ain't the only thing he's tried t' ruin. So she better never downplay my son again.

"But actually she made a fool a me, Miss Craig. After the argument I needed somethin' t' do. I felt so empty inside. I thought a takin' a taxi for a ride but I didn't even feel like ridin'.

"So I called Frankie t' say I wanta move. But he says why should we run? He says, 'Don't hate people just because a one.' An' he says, 'Lissen, hon, in a sense you act like a child. You better start learnin' t' toughen up. They're not happy people so the hell with them.' He says t' be polite, but real friendship is hard t' find. So from now on I'll stay by myself, 'cept for comin' here, I mean.

"But I bet if Frankie ever sees her on the sidewalk, he'd like t' give her ass a little kick. Frankie's got no pity for rats. So I know he hates her now . . . Still it hurts me real deep just the same. She wasn't no friend at all, just askin' me over t' talk about her car."

On the last full day of work before my August vacation, I went to see Matt and Nancy. Even out in the hall before I reached the office, I heard a strange thumping.

"Come in," Nancy yelled when I knocked. "I can't get to the door." She had Matt pinned on the floor, her knee on his chest, her hands holding his, spread-eagled. She put her face inches from his.

"I won't let you break that window," she yelled. He raised his head as high as he could, and spat in her eye. She spat back at him.

"I'll give it right back to you, mister, whatever you dish out." He rolled his head back, eyes closed, and screamed.

"You don't like that, huh? Then—no spitting! . . . Now." She rested back on her heels, still in kneeling position. "Think I can let you up?" His arms began flailing so fast the motion was a blur.

"No hurting yourself, you know I won't let you punch your head." She bent forward to restrain him. Like a frantic bicyclist, he kicked in circles until he struck her elbow with his heel.

"Ouch!" Nancy rocked back, holding her arm. I went to help her.

"No hurting, Matt," I said. "Not yourself or anyone else."

He beat his head a few more seconds, then rose to sitting position, as if he were waking up. "Wun?" he shook his head like he was dazed. "Doo? Dree?" Dull, lifeless, his eyes stared straight ahead.

"That's right. You can count. Good for you, Matt. You remember, don't you?" I was impressed with his perception. In the midst of a tantrum, he could distinguish my voice.

Nancy, fully recovered, rearranged small blocks on the table where Matt worked. "Let's show Mrs. Craig how we count the blocks." He went right to the chair and sat beside her.

I'd seen it so many times—children way out of control, able to pull themselves together to do a structured task.

"May I have three?" She cupped her hand. He picked them up one at a time, stopping with the third.

"Okay! Now I'd like five." She dropped the three she held. He offered her exactly five. I watched, delighted.

"Good, Matt!" She ran her hand through his straggly red hair.

"Now let's see you repeat the patterns." Using about ten blocks, she outlined a triangle. He duplicated it immediately.

"Okay, this time I'll take mine away." She formed a large "M", then swept the blocks into her lap.

He repeated it perfectly, even to the colors of blocks. "What a good memory you have!" Nancy spoke over her shoulder to me. "He's really terrific at this.

"Okay Matt, go draw on the blackboard. I know you've wanted to all week." He scribbled what looked like mountains left to right, the length of the ten-foot board, then began again from the other end. Nancy and I sat on the edge of the table, watching.

"I feel pretty mean about what I was doing when you came in. Fighting a little kid." Her voice sounded shaky. "But all week he's been trying to jump through that window. Runs toward it with his arms out like he's diving into a pool. I get terrified that I might not catch him in time. He's tried it once a day since I stopped bringing his mother."

"It's pretty rough on you," I sympathized.

"Well, I guess it's worse today. I'm either tired or coming down with something. And that makes everything harder." She blotted beads of moisture from her upper lip.

"Hey, I'm worried about you." Her forehead felt cold and moist. "You don't look at all well. Let me take Matt home for you, please. You just leave. Go home and rest."

"I—I'd really appreciate that." She swayed slightly, trying to reach her purse on the top of the locker.

"Are you sure you can drive?" I was alarmed.

"Sure," she smiled weakly. "Don't worry about me. Bye-bye Matt." He kept scribbling on the board after her car had left. I watched, absently wishing I'd taken him and followed Nancy, to be sure she was all right.

Matt had made a rectangle about twelve inches long and was grunting "Um, um—um—" as he drew tiny marks inside. His concentration surprised me. He worked at least five minutes in one spot.

"Miss Kelly had to go, Matt. I'm going to take you home." I walked toward him.

"My God!" I said out loud, not believing what I saw. Unevenly, but clearly, he'd printed J-E-O-P-A-R-D-Y in the rectangle! I wanted to run out and call someone, anyone, in to see it.

"Matt, do you know that word?" Who would believe he even knew one letter?

I put one arm around his waist, and pointed to his word with the other. "Can you read it?" I felt desperate to know. Could he communicate by writing—this child who couldn't talk?

"Look, Matt, do you know what it says?"

He focused his gaze on my forehead, his sad, lifeless blue eyes again avoiding mine. His mouth was drawn in a tight thin line—the lips didn't move.

"Matt." I wanted to shake him from his

dreamlike posture. "It says 'jeopardy'! That's what you wrote!"

He didn't even blink.

"Look." I printed his name on the board. "That's you, Matt, do you understand?"

He didn't look. I turned his chin with my hand, but he wouldn't even glance at the blackboard.

Maybe he'd respond to a treat. "Okay, my friend. For printing a word, you're getting a reward." If Nancy kept crackers, they were nowhere in the closet.

Matt stood exactly as I'd left him, chalk in his hand, eyelids half lowered.

"Guess what, Matt? No treats in here, so you and I are going out." I flicked out the lights, led him by the hand and locked the door behind us.

Dairy Queen seemed the wisest choice since we wouldn't have to go in. I ordered him a grape drink, not sure he'd feed himself anything solid. I sat him beside me on the picnic bench and thought about what he'd done, the word he'd written. I felt completely mystified. Could it have been purely rote memory, a repetition of patterns he'd seen on TV but couldn't decode? Or did he have some awareness of the word at least as a symbol, whether or not he knew its meaning? In either case I could hardly wait to let Nancy know.

Even his standing on the bench didn't distract me from my reverie. I sat dreaming until I felt the cold soda on my scalp, trickling down the back of my neck and spreading over both shoulders. My new white Indian blouse now had a sprawling purple yoke. Little square ice cubes perched on my head.

"Eee! Eee!" He tossed the paper cup onto the pavement and danced a left-foot, right-foot hop on our jiggly bench. Three men in suits glanced at me in disgust. "Permissive parents!" one said. A young mother scooped up her toddler and hurried to her car.

But somehow I didn't feel angry. Foolish, perhaps, and cold and wet, but not even a grape shower diminished the excitement I felt about his writing a word.

"Well, sir—" I looked up at him as I picked the ice cubes out of my hair. "You certainly celebrated, didn't you?"

"Eee! Eee!" He waved his arms as though he were conducting an orchestra and continued his dance. It was the first time I'd seen him looking really happy.

On the way home, he hummed and rocked himself contentedly on the seat until we turned down his own road. Suddenly he pushed forward, to the edge of the seat, nose pressed against the windshield.

"Bye now," he said, like a parrot. "Bye now." Then more and more anxiously: "Bye now—bye now—bye now," he repeated over and over, his voice rising to a shriek.

"Matt, you're almost home. Don't be afraid." I put my hand on his as he gripped the dashboard. As soon as we stopped, he rushed out and ran to his mother, who sat waiting on the steps. I thought she'd come over and ask why Nancy wasn't driving, but she turned immediately and took him into the house, slamming the door behind her.

We closed the office early that afternoon for our annual staff picnic. Several others besides myself would be on vacation in August. One of the social workers belonged to a beach club which owned Pleasure Island on Lake Pearl. She arranged for us to picnic there.

We sat outside at long tables with platters of fried chicken, macaroni salad and brownies. I wondered if our patients would have been surprised by our private conversations—light-hearted at first, then shared concerns about our own teen-agers.

"Look," one of the psychologists said, "it's their life. So let them live it."

"You can't really do that," his wife remarked.

I joined the first group leaving the island in the cramped outboard motorboat. It took ten minutes to chug across the bay. The evening star appeared just after a coral sunset.

At the dock we said goodbye for a month. Farewell to children mending, people tending. It was our turn to mend, for thirty days.

My first days of vacation were exactly as I'd planned. I reorganized bureaus and closets, overdue tasks which gave me a sense of well-being. The children painted the walls in Bill's office. We decided to spend a few days on the Cape as soon as the jobs were done. Bill was now in Israel for several weeks, doing research and interviews.

On Thursday, Nancy Kelly called. "My mother told me you'd tried to get me. I had the flu. This was my first day back to work since I saw you."

Barely waiting to hear she was well, I poured out the details of Matt's accomplishment. "I left it on the board for you to see."

"I just can't believe it! What a word for him to choose," she marveled. "Do you think he and his mother watch 'Jeopardy' on TV? But even so, how could he remember that many letters? And if he has no idea it's really a word, he's got a better memory and more ability than I'd ever guessed."

"I've had this strange thought, Nancy, that maybe he wrote 'jeopardy' to let us know that's how he really feels."

"Like a cry for help?" she asked slowly. "Mmm. That's fascinating. Especially now, with what I've got to tell you. I'm afraid my work with him is finished, and I don't even know why. I went to pick him up today, my first time after being sick. He and his mother weren't outside, like they've always been. When I honked the horn she yelled out a window not ever to come back again. 'My son's stayin' home,' she said."

"Oh no!" I felt terribly disappointed. We

couldn't lose this child at such a crucial time. "I'll try to reach her, Nancy. We can't give up on him now."

But when I telephoned her, Nellie was adamant. "I got used t' havin' him home after she cheated him outta them days. I don't believe her, sayin' that she was sick. He's not goin' back with that hussy. She's nothin' but a liar. My son's stayin' home with me."

"Nellie, I know for a fact Miss Kelly was ill. And Matt really needs to finish off the summer there. He's been doing so well . . ."

"Yah? By the talk of her at first my son was doin' good." Her voice was syrupy. "But last week she tole me he broke some of their stinkin' toys!" Now the words were spat in rage. "Well, ain't that tooo bad! So, what'sa matter with her? I don't need nobody sayin' my son's destructible. Don't she know how t' glue them things t'gether?" She became more defensive, more venomous, when I urged her to change her mind.

"Lissen, Frankie says we'll get a lawyer if anybody don't agree. A parent got a right t' make decisions." I could imagine how quickly Matt would regress, being locked in that house again. But instead of convincing her, my arguments fired her wrath.

"Well, I'm very sorry that's your decision, because I don't believe it's in Matt's best interest." I wanted her to feel my disapproval. If our relationship had any meaning, perhaps she'd reconsider; so I intentionally sounded distant. "Take care, Nellie. Call if you change your mind."

Ellen and Billy were loading the car for our trip. I was giving the house a final check—stove off, windows shut, iron unplugged—when the phone rang.

"Miss Craig?" I was surprised to hear her voice. "The reason I'm callin', see, ya tole me I could call, an' this is a real 'mergency. A guy outside says he's supposed t' clean the furnace. Now I'm scared that that ain't the truth, but he come with a big oil truck so maybe he ain't lyin'. D' ya think I should let him in?"

I didn't want this responsibility just when I was leaving. "Why don't you check with Frankie?"

She called back a few minutes later, sounding relaxed and pleased. "Aw, he's awful nice. He's down there at the furnace with some kinda vacuum. He looked right in my face when he came in. An' I got my yellow sweater on t'day. You know how some sweaters make you look big up there even though there ain't much behind it? Well that's how I look up top t'day.

"Frankie tole me call the cops if he starts any funny stuff. But I don't wanna get him in trouble, even though I can't stand no man near me, 'cept for Frankie, I mean."

It drizzled the first few days on the Cape, so we found a whaling museum, an aquarium with a dolphin show and some great fried clams. Thursday the sun came out, and Ann and Richie went off with friends. Billy, Ellen and I discovered a nearly deserted beach with thunderous waves and undulating sand dunes.

The kids explored while I stretched out on a beach towel and surrendered my mind to a stream of random thoughts. I wondered whether Bill's interviews for his book were working out successfully. I thought of the kids and each one's plans for the fall. Ann wanted to work a year instead of returning to college. I'd resisted, afraid that she might not go back to graduate. But she was certain she wanted other learning experiences outside the college walls, and she hoped to earn enough money for a trip to Africa.

I also thought of how things were usually hectic at the clinic in September and October. School social workers and guidance counsellors would begin calling daily, referring children about whom they were concerned. First we'd hear about the "acting-outers," whose behavior was most intolerable. Strangely, even these kids often exerted enough control to lull their teachers with a "honeymoon period" each September, although it rarely lasted longer than the month.

I wondered what new cases I'd be assigned and whether I'd be able to leave myself the time I'd need for some writing I hoped to do.

The sun was making me drowsy. My last thoughts, before drifting off to sleep, were of Matt and how we might help him. Next week, I promised myself, I'll call Leora.

We were barely in the door the day we got home when the phone rang.

"Mrs. Craig? Charles Perlwitz from Protective Service here." The words were clipped, the deep voice grave. "Got your name from the town school office. Social worker there, a—uh—Mrs. Black, said I should talk to you. Sorry to call you at home, but you know we're obliged to act quickly. Now I understand you're working with the family I'm calling about—Barringer?"

"Barringer?" Why would Protective Service be involved with them, I wondered. "Well yes, but . . ."

"We need all the informaton that's pertinent about the boy. Got a report of suspected child abuse."

"I don't understand." I was truly startled. "Who reported them for that?"

"A Lieutenant Robert Megan of the Concord Police. But the original complaint was made by an oil-burner service man. Went to the Barringer house to clean the furnace. Poor guy walks down the basement and shines his flashlight on the burner, but while he's doing it he notices—uh—piles of—uh—excrement all over the floor. Guess you can imagine how he felt. Thought they must have a dog or somethin'. Then this naked kid comes running out of the shadows, screaming his head off, and squats to relieve himself right on the floor. The guy was terrified.

"He drove his truck right to the police station, and that's when Lieutenant Megan called us in on this child-abuse charge. Now I held off till I talked to you because I understand the family's getting help. But you know we have to investigate this."

I knew that the implications of such an investigation were very serious. Overburdened, the state worker would have little time for the unique aspects of a single case. Nor was that his responsibility. He was simply to determine whether the current living arrangement was in the best interests of the child. This would be seen as a clear case of neglect.

I paused, wondering if I could or should convince him not to interfere right now. How could I expect him to appreciate the potential for growth I'd seen in this child?

I decided to plead for time. "Mr. Perlwitz, I think I know the circumstances of this report. If you'd trust me to do the investigating, I'll get back to you right away. I know it sounds like gross neglect, but I assure you the child's in no imminent danger of physical abuse."

"Well, I don't know what you call abuse, Mrs. Craig. I never heard of anything like this before," he said sarcastically. "The parents live fine but they keep the kid in the basement like an animal. Is that your story?"

"The parents are workable and the boy is retarded, but he's not hopeless." I realized my voice was rising and swallowed hard before I went on. "And no matter what his parents are doing wrong, Mr. Perlwitz, you won't find a foster home to take this boy. He'd go to the state institution for the retarded, and you know what would happen to him there as well as I do. He'd have less care in that place than he's getting now.

"If he's sent there he won't have a chance, and I have a feeling, if we could just have some time, there could be a breakthrough soon—both with the child and with his parents."

There was a long silence on the other end of the phone. Glancing out the window I saw a group of boys Matt's age playing ball. I felt a lump rising in my throat.

"All right," he sighed finally. "I'll hold onto this case until I've heard from you. We'll wait three days for your written report. You know I shouldn't, but—ah—I know how it feels when you've already gotten involved . . ."

"Mr. Perlwitz, thank you."

"Okay, it's a deal. But—ah—Mrs. Craig? There's one more thing I'd like to say . . ."

"Yes?"

"Listen—ah—just don't go breakin' your heart on these cases . . ."

If Mr. Perlwitz had taken over the Barringer

case, he would have visited their home unannounced to get the clearest sense of what was going on. And so, I felt, should I. I woke to the first rainy day after a week of balmy weather. By midmorning the downpour was so intense that my old Buick kept stalling on the short trip to Burley Street.

I parked by the fence and sat in the car a moment while the rain beat furiously on the roof. Why, I wondered, did I feel such an ominous impact from this place, which looked so much like the other shingled ranches on the road? The darkened windows contributed to the feeling that something was wrong in this particular house.

The rain let up a bit and I made a dash for the gate, finding with relief that it hadn't been locked. Still, my hair got soaked in the short run across the yard. I knocked on the door, but no one answered. Finally, dripping and shivering, I began to pound with my fist. Still not a sound from within. Then I noticed the curtain in the middle window being drawn back, just as it had been on my first trip here. I was guardedly watching the window, when the door in front of me was suddenly flung wide open.

She stood barefoot, clutching the neckline of her light blue bathrobe. Her eyes were sunken in smoke-colored shadows, her auburn hair matted in snarls.

"I'm sorry if I woke you up." I began to step inside. "I thought no one was home."

"Now ain't that dumb!" she whispered hoarsely. "I never woulda answered the door if I was out! Hey!" She blocked the entrance with her arm. "Where d' ya' think you're goin'?"

"Can't I come in, Nellie? I need to talk to you."

"About what?" She moved grudgingly. "Whatever ya' come t' talk about, just spit it out quick, 'cause my son's still sleepin'."

It was so dark in the house that at first I could see only a blurred white form across the room. Then the form shifted, and I recognized a sheet draped over a figure on the couch. The boy murmured as his bare arm dangled to the floor. He groped around until his hand came to rest on a partially filled baby bottle. Picking it up, he turned toward the wall and gurgled noisily on the nipple.

I wondered why the room should be so dark. What was covering the windows? There were no ceiling fixtures, lamps, or tables to hold the lamps. The one source of light in the room came from the flickering TV, left on without the sound. The only other pieces of furniture, besides the TV and the couch, were two plastic kitchen chairs side by side in front of the television.

"Lissen—" Her hisslike whisper intruded on my surveillance. "My son don't like no strangers comin' here."

"Are you telling me I'm still a stranger?" I smiled, hoping to display more confidence than I felt.

She stared at me. "The way I figger," she snapped back, "this here is my son's home, an' I

respect his right t' want nobody comin' in, stranger
or no stranger."

"And maybe you feel the same way, too." I
was no longer smiling. "But, Nellie, I haven't come
here just to visit. There's something awfully important we've got to talk about . . ."

"Here?" she looked around frantically. "Oh
no! Not here! This ain't no place for talkin'. Lissen,
me an' my son, we was plannin' t' come to your
office some one a these days." She stepped forward,
forcing me back against the door. "We'll take one a
them taxis." Her voice kept rising. "Next week,
okay?" She looked up at me from under a lock of
tangled hair, as if she were checking whether I
believed her.

The child began to whimper and stir. She
went to him and pulled the sheet over his naked
arm. I saw that her hands were trembling.

"I'm sorry my being here upsets you," I said
softly, "but Nellie, what I need to say can't wait. So
do you want to talk in here," I nodded toward Matt,
"or in some other room?"

"It can't wait, huh?" Biting her lower lip,
she, too, glanced at the boy, then back at me. "We
just ain't used t' company here. That's all." Sigh-
ing, she pushed the door shut, then padded barefoot to yet another dark room. I watched her
silhouette as she groped toward the ceiling until she
caught the string dangling from the light fixture.
Suddenly, two harsh naked bulbs illuminated the
tiny kitchen, which was painted shocking pink.
Each wall was curiously marred by white blotches

where someone had tried to wash the garish pink paint. Gradually, I realized the reason it was so dark: The windows had been boarded over with sheets of plywood.

By now she'd regained her composure and was eyeing me suspiciously. "So how come you're bustin' in my house—so bossy about it—like you an' me ain't never been friends?"

"Hey, that's just why I came, Nellie, because I do feel like we're friends. And I want to tell you something that's going on. Could we sit together?" I pulled out one of the chairs at the pink oval table.

"Go ahead," she nodded, "go ahead an' sit if ya hafta. You—you wanna cuppa coffee?" She lifted the lid of a battered aluminum percolator on top of the stained white stove. "Frankie made it early this mornin'. It oughta taste okay.

"You like it with sugar? Huh?" She scurried to a cupboard and brought out a chipped white bowl. "Yes, I bet you do take sugar. Is it somethin' 'bout my son that's goin' on? 'Cause me an' Frankie knows our rights, ya know." Her eyes kept darting anxiously in my direction. "An' no one can make us send him t' school. You take milk, too? Is that what it's all about?" Finally, with cautious, sliding steps, she carried both steaming mugs of coffee to the table and sank into the other chair.

"Okay," I began, "I'll explain as well as I can. Yesterday I got a call from a social worker in Protective Service." I was choosing the words carefully. "That's an agency of the state that . . ."

"Wait a minute! I forgot the milk!" She

jumped up and took a half-gallon carton out of the refrigerator. "See this here ice chest?" I thought she was pointing to the deep dents on the outside of the refrigerator. It looked as though it had been hammered or kicked countless times.

Instead, she opened the door and gestured to the crammed shelves inside. "'Member I tole you how my brother Calvin usta steal stuff after our mother died? Well, that's how come I keep so much food in here right now. An' Frankie, he don't mind at all, ya know. He remembers bein' hungry, too."

Once she put the milk carton on the table, her voice hardened. "So what's the name of the bums been askin' 'bout me an' my son?"

"Let me just finish about Protective Service, Nellie. They have to get involved, even on the slightest suspicion of child abuse."

"Well they got a point there," she nodded. "I dunno who tole 'em, but that kid really does abuse things. You can see for yourself if you look around. But I ain't gonna tell them people my son's destructible, Miss Craig, even though he's almost kicked in my whole refrigerator and smashed out every one a them windows. That's why Frankie covered them with wood. He says he ain't gonna fix them with glass no more.

"Oh." She jumped up. "There goes that stinkin' cat! Gives a person a headache openin' an' closin' the door so much."

I hadn't heard the cat; but when she opened the kitchen door, a scrawny orange animal darted across the room and down a dark hall. "Filthy thing ain't no company at all, like Frankie promised."

"Nellie." She'd sat down again, but I felt I had to get her attention quickly before there was another distraction. "I know you're worried about what I've come to say, but let me start again. In a way, a report to Protective Service can be a kind of warning to the family. You see, when they talk about child abuse they mean either someone hurting a child, or not giving him proper care."

"Anyone says I hurt my son's a liar!" she yelled. "I ain't never done nothin' t' him like that. An' if them bums from the state think they're takin' him away"—purple splotches began to break out on her neck—"if anyone thinks somethin' like that"—grabbing her spoon, she pointed the handle toward me as if it were a knife—"you can tell 'em for me I'll cut their guts right out!"

"Now listen, Nellie," my voice rose, too, "I know how much you care for Matt . . ."

But she'd dropped the spoon and turned away. Following her gaze I saw him standing on the threshold between the kitchen and the living room. He was completely naked, with both his hands concealed behind his back. Blinking from the harsh light, his eyes flicked over my face, then focused on the wall above my head. Slowly, he arched his left arm back until his hand was straight up over his head. Something dark was cupped in his fist.

I'd barely ducked when the handful of excrement sailed by, splattering the wall precisely behind where I'd sat. Stunned, I stared at the mess, then turned back to the boy. He was raising his right arm in the same pitching motion. I crouched again but this time he aimed lower. Most of it hit the floor, but bits of feces splattered up on my shoes and slacks. I stood there, numbed by the shock and the terrible smell.

Matt tilted his head quizzically, then broke into a wide grin, turned and ran away. I caught a glimpse of his mother, smirking at the stains on my slacks. Then I had to close my eyes to conquer the waves of nausea and tears of indignation.

"I tole ya!"—her tone was mocking—"I tole ya Matt don't want no company here. Ya' can't say nobody never warned ya."

Still sickened, I got up and headed toward the dark living room. Matt was lying on his back in the middle of the floor. As I walked around his naked body, he drew his knees to his chest and urinated on his stomach. Then, giggling softly, he began to rock on his back.

By the time I reached the door, my whole body was trembling. I glanced a last time at each of them. Matt on the floor, laughing louder. His mother, leaning against the sink, eyeing me coldly over the mug of coffee she'd raised to her lips. How could I possibly have felt any hope for either of them?

"I came here thinking—" I knew I shouldn't be shouting, but they'd finally gotten to me"— foolishly thinking you cared enough about your son to stop this craziness between you, but I can see how wrong I was!"

Eyes narrowed, she continued to stare at me, then slowly turned her back and noisily sipped her coffee.

I let the door slam as I ran out across the yard, eager to put as much distance as possible between myself and those two. Then I stopped by my car and stood in the rain so that the raindrops would rinse the ugly stains from my clothes.

But even outside, I could still hear Matt's manic giggle; and I realized his mother, too, was enjoying my predicament. No rainfall could cool my searing indignation.

As soon as I got home, I pulled two towels from the drier and was heading for a shower when the phone rang.

"Look—" He didn't identify himself but I recognized the angry voice. "I know I asked for your help," Nellie's husband said, "but now you've gone too far. That's movin' in on my wife's territory, see, when you start goin' into the home."

"I wonder if you understand, Mr. Barringer, why I went to your house today?" I felt cold toward this man who once had begged me to visit their home. "We got a report of child abuse—and that's a terribly serious charge. Let me tell you honestly, Mr. Barringer, the state considered taking Matt out of your home. And I put myself on the line for you. I said 'no' because I really thought you people cared enough to want to change."

"She told me all a that," he said bitterly, "and it just don't scare me at all. Like I warned you before, she's been tricked and cheated too many times. It ain't gonna happen again. I'll move them right outta state before any one a youse workers snatch my kid."

"I remember something you said in the beginning, Mr. Barringer, about helping Matt as much as possible."

"Well, I changed my mind since then. I used t' think I wanted them both more into the world, but I was wrong about that. Some people ain't meant t' be out in the world."

"Children aren't meant to be locked in houses!" I was really angry now.

"Listen, one a the gentlemen comes in this here laundry happens t' be a lawyer, see." He paused to clear his throat and his voice returned deeper and firmer. "An' he's been advisin' me, so t' speak, on just what a parent got in the way of rights. An' you can tell the state t' either lay off the Barringers or we might be startin' t' sue. Just tell them workers they can only push a man so far."

"Workers can only be pushed so far, too," I said, "and the state worker felt the situation at your home was critical. You're not being realistic, Mr. Barringer. If things don't change quickly for Matt, what happens to him may be out of your control."

Chapter 10

I T was Friday night of Labor Day weekend. My son Billy's band was playing downtown at the Youth-Adult Center. Richard and Ellen were helping him set up sound equipment. I'd just waved goodbye to Ann, who was driving to Providence to sublet her apartment. She'd definitely decided to take a semester off to earn some money for a trip.

I expected to write the Protective Service report quickly and mail it on my way to catch the last of Billy's songs. There seemed little doubt about what to write: a decisive request that the Barringer child be removed from his home. I'd have to admit I was wrong. The basic maternal bond which ought to make a situation workable was too destructive there.

What chance did he have, after what I'd seen, to function in any capacity unless he were taken away—rescued at once from parents who found some strange gratification in keeping their child a primitive? Perhaps they could visit him, but he could no longer live with them.

Yet, again I thought of the stark realities that had prompted me to urge Mr. Perlwitz not to take immediate action. If it were possible that a nurturing foster home—or even a well-run treatment center—would accept Matt now, I wouldn't have wavered. But neither was true. There were long waiting lists for children who functioned much better than he—children who'd be considered more worthy of the state's investment.

At Matt's age and condition of relative primitiveness, he'd be sent to the Center for Retarded Citizens. Housed in a forbidding Victorian building, it had recently been the focus of a nightmarelike series of television editorials. The pictures flashed through my mind: naked children languishing in cribs; lying in scum on the bathroom floor; outside in snow, wrapped only in sweaters. Stories of cruel discipline. The pathetic testimony of a retarded teen-ager allowing the interviewer to examine his bruises.

Being locked behind the brick walls of a poorly-funded, understaffed institution was not the way for Matt to escape neglect. I just couldn't relegate him to that kind of a future. His parents did care, however inappropriately, and that meant something.

What choice was there, really, but to try again, harder than before, to strengthen the home, to break the unwholesome bonds between these people. They *had* come for help. Perhaps it shouldn't be me, but someone else who'd have to start all over.

And so I wrote to Mr. Perlwitz asking him to allow our agency to continue to assess the suitability of the Barringer home and report our findings to him every three months for a year. I dreaded the thought of contacting them again; but maybe Ceil Black, or someone else less involved than I, could convince them that time was running out for Matt. The longer they rejected outside help the less chance there'd be of its making any difference.

I hoped that since they now knew the state could threaten them with his removal, it would force them to accept a day program or some educational plan. Ceil Black knew more about educational resources than I did. I'd call her on Wednesday, my first day back at work.

But Ceil knew of nothing. "The only really appropriate day program," she said, "would be the Regional Developmental Center some of the area towns have been planning. But that won't be ready for several months, if then. They're still negotiating to remodel the old convent building down by Lake Pearl."

Years before, Ceil and I had worked together on a pilot program for socially and emotionally maladjusted children. From it sprang a variety of classes for perceptually handicapped, neurologically impaired, and emotionally disturbed. Then came the trend toward "mainstreaming." Not one self-contained special class for nonretarded had survived the shift.

With extra support from a "learning center" one hour a day, advocates of mainstreaming claimed, schools could eliminate the stigma of placing a child in a special class. And for many children, learning centers were enough. But other children appeared even more bizarre and further isolated when they were added to a larger group.

Some lacked the inner control to contain their anxiety and rage. Their classmates became their victims. We failed, I felt, not only the victims, but also their aggressors, by placing them in situations which provoked their lack of impulse control.

"Throwing the baby out with the bath water," Ceil had called it. "So now we have to start all over again, only it's regional instead of on a local level. And that means busing emotionally disturbed kids for miles on end. Anyway," she sighed, "there's no existing group for Matt, and no date when there will be. All we can do now is put him on a waiting list for when the new school opens and, until then, pay a tutor to work with him an hour a day."

That was a start, and there seemed to be no alternative. Ceil agreed to present it to the Barringers. I'd had no contact with them since that dreadful visit. I was, in fact, relieved at the prospect of putting their case in her hands. I saw no way that

I could any longer be effective with this mother and child.

Ceil put Matt's name on the waiting list for the Regional Developmental Center. She was also, I assumed, looking for a tutor to work with Matt one hour each day.

Dr. Diamond had to leave early on Thursday, September twelfth, so our noontime staff meeting had just been canceled when Ceil called my office with an offer of lunch.

"Chiliburgers, french fries. You name it—I'll treat." "Can't resist a chiliburger," I said, "especially if we agree not to talk about work."

We got take-out orders of coffee, french fries and hamburgers loaded with chili—a treat I never tired of—and sat in Ceil's Ford in front of the "Thunderbird," a local teen-age hangout. Juggling the food in the cramped space, we began by chatting about our families. I told her Ann's plans; she talked about her husband and child. Every few minutes we had to raise our voices over the sound of gunning motors, as young drivers roared in and out of the parking lot.

There was a moment of silence while Ceil dipped the last french fry into the final bit of catsup.

"El—I really want to talk about something else—" She paused again for a sip of coffee, but her voice was so intent I looked up at her in surprise. "Is there any chance that we—the Board of Ed, I mean—could hire you to do that tutoring with Matt?"

"Oh, Ceil, I wish you wouldn't ask . . ." I stopped for a moment, thinking of what that commitment would mean. "There's some writing I've been trying to get done. And besides, my last experience with the Barringers was so wearing, I don't think I want to put myself in that position again. Somehow I've let myself be too vulnerable." I stopped to think of the amount of time and energy this family had taken. "Maybe I was hoping for too much. Anyway, I've decided to cut myself off from the case completely, and . . ."

"Look, I realize how much you cared, and I know it makes things all the harder, but that's exactly why we need you now. Besides, who else can deal with his mother?"

"But I can't do that anymore either. That's just what I'm trying to tell you, Ceil . . ."

"El, the real bind is—not only is no one else available, but she won't accept anyone but you. She really likes you, you know? Would you believe that when I told her Matt could have a tutor, she said you—you're her only worker, and her only friend, too. She insisted she'd kick out anyone else." I felt a rush of compassion, realizing that our harrowing contacts were as close as Nellie had come to a friendship.

"To tell the truth, El," Ceil fiddled with the key, "she's lodged a complaint against me because I haven't sent you over there already."

"A complaint? With whom?"

"She actually called the Superintendent of Schools. Hard to believe it's the same woman who didn't know how to dial!'' I had to chuckle trying to imagine those two conversing.

"What'd she say?"

"She said it's the superintendent's responsibility to have you tutor Matt and teach her son to talk. She told him the Board of Ed better stop 'sitting on its butt' because somebody's got the ball—and she and Frankie want him to find out who that person is."

"And how'd he answer that?" I pictured our stately silver-haired superintendent in his formal office trying to handle her raucous demands.

"By calling me to ask who the hell does have the ball."

We both laughed.

"It's amazing, isn't it," Ceil wiped her eyes, "that this woman could be so effective at getting what she wants. But the problem is that the superintendent got very upset. He's worried about the unfavorable publicity if anyone finds out we knew about this situation and didn't have an educational plan. You know how sensitive he is to that kind of criticism. He'd rather see that kid in the Center for Retarded Citizens than see himself be accused of doing nothing . . . You see, we don't have much choice.

"I'm planning to suggest Matt for the class of trainable retarded, but that can't happen till the Planning and Placement Team meets. The superintendent says we've got to offer them something right away. I know how wearing it will be, but I'd never beg you if I thought it would go on indefinitely. Would you give it an hour a day for just a few weeks?"

"Six weeks at most? You guarantee?" I'd known for a long time that the therapy of choice for Matt right now was "training and education." And I wanted, I realized, to play a part in ordering his world.

I missed teaching. Someday, perhaps, a therapist would be able to work with him on interpreting his inner life. But for now, he was too deficient in basic skills.

"Ceil, did his mother really ask for me? She hasn't been calling at all. It's been a welcome relief; my last visit there was such a disaster." I looked out at the litter of broken glass and paper containers strewn across the parking lot and remembered running from their house to my car on that unpleasant day—the last time I'd seen them.

"I know it was hard," Ceil sighed. "I guess I have no right to ask you to go back."

"What a technique!" I laughed. "You know I'm hooked. But you'll have to wait till I can make some time. It'll take a little juggling. But—hey—Ceil . . ."

"Yah?" She looked up.

"Please—no more of your free lunches."

She smiled and I got out and started walking to my car.

"Oh—I almost forgot!" She rolled down her window. "The superintendent wants a psychiatric reevaluation on that child—you know—to justify

the expense of tutoring him to the Board of Ed.
Would you handle the arrangements between Nellie and your clinic? I'll transport them there and
back."

"Okay, okay," I nodded. "How do you always manage to get me involved?"

"Simple." She grinned and turned on the
ignition key, letting the motor roar. "All I have to
do is ply you with a chiliburger."

Dr. Diamond, who'd seen Matt the first time
they came to the Center, agreed to do the reevaluation.

I felt nervous about talking to Nellie again,
but it was she who put me at ease when I called to
set the appointment for Thursday at three.

"Well hi ya, hon! So whatcha been doin'?
Hey hon—you sound like you got a cold. You
shoulda stayed in bed all day. Why don't ya take
one of them contracts for colds. I seen them on TV.
I don't want my son t' get a cold an' I tole that other
worker me an' my son won't talk t' no one but you.

"Say, ya know what that stinkin' cat done
this mornin'? Popped out a bunch of kittens—right
on my bed . . . So when ya comin' over, huh?
Honest, it ain't gonna be like that other time. It's
just we wasn't used t' company.

"Oh my sister tole me my brother's still
locked in that nut-house. Ya know the one went
streakin'? Well, they're keepin' him for offserva-
tion."

Those curious leaps in her mental process—less frequent when I'd gotten to know her—were more obvious, I realized again, when she was feeling uneasy.

"You oughta see them squealy things. Like little baby rats. I tole Frankie he oughta come home an' drown 'em all, but he's gonna ask down the laundry who wants a stinkin' cat. But in one sense, it hurts me the way Frankie's been downin' my brother. Says he probably been smoking that pop. I guess it's true what Frankie says, that I let myself get hurt. Everytime I try reachin' out t' my family, I keep findin' out again there really ain't nothin' there.

"Hey, Frankie's been talkin' 'bout Matt's bein' retarded and all. I know he ain't no doctor—workin' in that dirty laundry—but Frankie thinks it's us that held Matt back ourselves. So Frankie an' me'll bring him t' your doctor over there. An' don't think I'm downin' that doctor or nothin' cause I really don't even know him, but I don't get how he's gonna tell if Matt's brain's been damaged. You know yourself he won't sit down.

"Anyway, Frankie wants you t' teach my son anything at all. An' I do, too. Take care a that cold now. I missed ya, hon."

Although she'd tried to be casual when we'd made the appointment, Mrs. Barringer phoned six times from Monday to Wednesday, expressing her growing concern that she and Matt might have to see Dr. Diamond without Frankie.

"How'd I know what t' say when we got there? What if I don't know what t' do? . . . An' d'ya think that doctor remembers my son don't know how t' act?"

"I'd be surprised if he'd forgotten, Nellie."

"Think he'll be mad if Matt gets nasty? But I tole Frankie he hadda promise t' drive us there. I'd be too nervous 'bout seein' that man alone."

I was with a patient, so Sylvia took the final message.

"Tell Craigie my husband's such a big shot now—sure—he'll valenteer t' open an' close that stinkin' laundry—but he can't drive us to the 'kiatrist."

Dick and I were waiting by the receptionist's desk when their taxi drove up at ten to three. Minutes ticked by, but no one left the cab.

"Shall I go out and see what's going on?" I asked.

"She might as well face me now. You know," he headed for the door, "some of my patients come running in to see me."

She didn't even notice me standing there when the three paraded by. Her lips were clenched, her eyes riveted on Dr. Diamond's back as he loped ahead. Matt was screaming in her arms, like he'd done so many times before. His cries faded as they moved up the stairs; but Doug, who'd passed them, shook his head in annoyance when he walked into the main office.

"That noise just isn't fair to the rest of our patients. Or to me, either," he added.

Doug and I and the rest of the staff had gathered for a three-thirty meeting when we heard them leave. Leora, who was speaking, had to stop until Matt's screams finally faded. Doug looked disgusted.

Dr. Diamond was gone by the time we were through, but Sylvia handed me his dictation early the next day.

BARRINGER, MATT
PSYCHIATRIC EVALUATION

Mother and Matt were seen together. Stepfather was unable to leave work, a fact which mother announced with some bitterness. At the time of the clinical appointment, both mother and Matt were sitting outside in a taxi, as though there were some confusion. This examiner went out to investigate. When Matt saw the examiner approaching he clung tightly to his mother, burying his head in her shoulder while uttering a loud, high-pitched scream. The mother claimed that she needed help because of the child's anxiety about coming into the building. I suspect she, too, was afraid.

When they were finally in the playroom Matt sat on his mother's lap facing her with his legs astride her lap, his head still buried in her shoulder. He screamed constantly in a high-pitched voice, although toward the end of the interview he periodically sneaked a look at the examiner. Although mother responded that she has seen tears in his eyes, the examiner did not observe any tearing despite his cries.

Impression: Matt is a six-year, nine-month-old Caucasian boy referred for behavior problems. He presents extreme separation anxiety, poor frustration tolerance, marked limitation in use of language, intense clingingness to his mother, apparent inability to be toilet trained or weaned from the bottle.

This is a complex case. Clearly there is significant retardation and unevenness in the boy's level of functioning, in addition to his intense anxiety. Therefore the problem becomes one of determining the extent and primacy of organic as opposed to psychological factors.

The severity of his difficulty, the intensity of his anxiety, the shrillness of his cry all might suggest that Matt's primary problem is of organic etiology, probably of congenital origin.

While some of the psychological difficulties could occur secondary to an organic disorder, it must be kept in mind that the clinical picture might also result from extreme overinfantilization, the possibility of a severely traumatic early life experience, or severe early deprivation.

Diagnosis:
1. Developmental deviation, severe, in a pre-latency-age boy with a history of maternal overindulgence.
2. Organic or congenital factors or a neurological condition of a progressively deteriorating nature. Possibly a fixed cerebral lesion.
3. Autistic traits with retardation.
4. Childhood schizophrenia.

Prognosis: Poor. This boy is not a candidate for a regular public school program. He will require a special placement and a prolonged evaluation to further clarify our understanding of this complex case. There is, as yet, no clear definition as to the etiology of his difficulty.

Recommendation:
1. Neurological evaluation to clarify the organic aspect when this can be realistically accomplished in an effective manner. At present, since there is no overt problem such as seizures, neurological tests

would not be likely to be of much value in making initial educational plans.

2. Mrs. Barringer must have further supportive counselling to aid her in more successful management of Matt. Stepfather should be involved as often as possible.
3. Again, there will have to be a prolonged evaluation of this case.

I was startled by the subtle change in this evaluation from earlier thoughts about Matt. Dr. Diamond was shifting the focus from organic causes to the possibility of early deprivation or overinfantilization. Was it possible that Matt could have been born with the potential for near normal development? The thought filled me with sadness. It was easier to accept his having suffered organic damage.

I was both surprised and relieved not to hear from Nellie for several days after she and Matt had seen the psychiatrist. I didn't want to deal with her until I was ready to tutor Matt. But when she finally called, she sounded enraged. "Boy, that doctor of yours is really a doozy! I don't want him as a doctor at all."

I tried to get her to be more specific, but she continued to rant. "He don't like t' talk on the phone at all. I said t' him—what's wrong with him—'cause he oughta be there when I need him. But he just ain't polite. I'd rather talk t' you."

Ten minutes later Dr. Diamond waved me

into his office. "Every day another question!" he raged through gritted teeth, shoving the phone almost off the desk. "'But I have t' talk t' the 'kiatrist—'" He mimicked Nellie's voice. "And I took her damn calls, thinking I could help with her kid! She never even mentions his name!

"No more!" he shook his fist at the phone. "I've had one too many interruptions from her. Oh God!" he said, sinking back against his chair, his hand across his forehead. "She's really got me raving!"

"Dick, I've never seen you so upset. What'd she say?"

"I'll tell you what she said. She insisted on knowing when I'd be able to pierce her ears. When I told her 'never,' she called me a stupid doctor not to do that kind of work."

"Look," I started giggling—then couldn't stop laughing—"I'm afraid I'll lose my earrings, Dick." I swept my hair back. "Unless you'd . . ."

"See you later, funny girl!" He motioned toward the door with his thumb. "No! Wait a minute. I want you to tell her any more phone calls will be charged to her account. And as soon as the boy is settled in a program, why don't you refer her elsewhere? Christian Charities—or whatever agency you choose.

"I want no more to do with her." He held up both hands, palms out, like he was pushing Nellie away. "And I think you should taper off too. No one can set limits on that woman. Just close this case as quickly as you can."

When the Board of Ed approved the funds for me to tutor Matt, Ceil called up urging me to begin. I felt a nagging concern about whether it was in Matt's best interest that I should tutor him after he'd come to me, first, at the clinic. I decided to phone Leora for her opinion.

"I understand your question," she said, "but with a child in such desperate need, who would criticize any plan that might help? Besides, Dr. Diamond doesn't think they belong at our clinic. And I'd agree. This sounds like a more appropriate plan.

"To me, the greater concern is how to prevent Mrs. Barringer from sabotaging your efforts. You'll have to remember it's you and not his mother who wants this boy to learn."

Leora's words prepared me once again to divide my attention between Nellie and Matt. I decided I'd try to involve her as a sort of teacher's aide.

I gave a lot of thought to how to work with Matt, especially where to begin. He had so little sense of himself as a separate being from his mother. I decided that we could stand before a mirror, retracing the steps he seemed to have missed in earliest childhood—the discovery of his hands and feet, hair, eyes, nose and mouth. I could help him learn the names of the parts of his body, in an effort to define himself as a person.

Then I reconsidered. Matt had clearly shown how difficult it was for him to make contact with people. I'd begin with inanimate objects. I knew he found things less threatening than people. We'd start with puzzles, records, toys with wheels.

But when I went to their house on Monday, Matt was asleep on the couch. And Nellie, still in her bathrobe, claimed she'd forgotten I was coming. "I was just about to have my coffee," she paused to yawn. "Would ya like t' have some, hon?"

As we tiptoed across the living room, Matt began to stir, his mouth working in a sucking motion. "That kid," she clucked, "always dreaming about takin' milk from his bottle."

She filled two mugs with coffee and we each carried one to the table. "Hey, what if you an' me just talk today, okay? I mean, my son's asleep, so who's gonna know if you don't teach him nothin'?"

"Okay with me." I shrugged, "I wanted to talk to you anyway—to get your ideas about where to start with Matt. I was thinking you and I could kind of work together."

"I ain't no teacher," she shot back. "You're the one that's s'posed t' be the teacher. Now the talkin' idea," her voice softened, "that's different. 'Cause I do need t' do some talkin'. At first, see—" she leaned closer, "at first I thought this tutorin' would be a good idea. But yesterday I saw this TV show about people havin' mental blocks in their head an' I knew that's what's wrong with my son. In other words, he got one a them blocks in his head and it won't go away till it's good and ready. So," she folded her arms and sat back smugly, "what could be the sense of you tutorin' him at all?"

"Maybe you're right," I nodded. "Maybe he's not ready to learn. But I've already been paid for a couple of weeks, so we might as well give it a try."

There was a heavy silence while Nellie took two sips of coffee, then toyed with the mug. "Ya know," she finally spoke, "I been thinkin' about you. An' feelin' kinda sorry for your kids."

I became guarded.

"Oh yeah," her eyes bore intently into mine. "I feel kinda sorry for them all. How many are there? Four? I bet they wish you never worked at all. 'Cause look at me. Enjoyin' bein' home with my son. An' they probably won't tell you so as not t' hurt your feelings."

"I think it's taught my kids responsibility," I said. "Of course my kids are older than Matt."

"An' what about your husband—huh? He must be resentful too. 'Cause what if all them wives in the world went out t' get jobs like you? An' all over the country, women stopped cleanin' their homes." The purplish blotches that came when she got upset had begun to appear on her neck and were spreading up to her face.

"I'll tell ya the answer! Then all them men

like Frankie would have t' go home to a filthy mess.
C'mon now Miss Craig," Her voice kept rising. "Ya
know that's true now don'tcha?"

I was getting annoyed. "Listen, Nellie, men
can help too—"

"Frankie says some women think marriage
is just ole fashioned now. An' that's why they
started that women's lip—'cause they're all r'bellin'
against bein' at home.

"Funny," she mused, "I usta think I oughta
be more like you. More out in the world, I mean.
An' now I feel kinda different, see. I'm home with
my kid 'cause that's what's right. An' you oughta be
home with yours."

I shook my head. "My kids and I can't stay
locked in the house together. Other people have to
help them learn. The very fact that I love them
means they have to be taught by other people,
who'll be more objective about what they do. Anyway, there's no way I can teach them all they'll
need to know. Life's too complicated for that."

But by now I felt drained by the effort it took
to deal with this woman. I'd had enough of her
transparent cunning and wanted to get up and go
home.

"I'm leaving now, Nellie. Please have Matt
up and dressed tomorrow at nine. I'd really like to
get him started."

"So you're comin' back!" She rose and
shook her head. "Well, I hope you'll wake up—
someday—to the embarrassing spot you put your-

self in. Ha," she chuckled sarcastically. "You oughta know more than that. Competitioning with men."

Again, the next morning the sheet was draped over the couch, but I was relieved to see that Matt wasn't under it.

"You ain't gonna mind if he ain't entirely dressed, now are ya?" His mother, still in her robe, glared at me angrily—my punishment, apparently, for asking that Matt be ready.

"An' you sure wouldn't mind if his little thing ain't covered, now would ya? I mean, after all, it ain't that big," she said sarcastically. "An' my son don't like wearin' no pants in his house. On accounta," she pointed, "he likes t' pee over there in that corner, so he don't wanta fuss with no pants."

The floorboards in the corner were warped and blackened.

"Yes I do mind, Nellie." I could hear the edge in my voice as I returned her glare. "I mind if Matt pees on that floor. I mind for you and I mind for him."

"Oh, it ain't that much. I can soak it up with a sponge."

"That's no answer at all! He's got to be trained if he's going to go to school." Suddenly there was the jarring clatter of dishes smashing—as though a heavily overstacked tray had fallen to the floor.

"You're gonna get it now," she screamed, rushing toward the commotion. Matt, naked except for a rumpled white undershirt, stood on the kitchen countertop giggling maniacally as he looked down at the bits of broken crockery all around his feet. He'd swept every dish and cup out of the cupboard. Everything was smashed. "Hee-hee-hee-hee." He balanced a triangular piece of china on his toes and began to raise his foot. "Hee-hee."

Nellie reached into the sink and picked a spatula out of the drainer. Brandishing it like a sword, she moved stealthily toward her son. "You're gettin' it now, boy, with this here panny cake turner. You're gonna get it now." When she was almost close enough to touch him he leapt to the floor, squealing excitedly, and ducked under her outstretched arms.

Grinning, her eyes gleaming, she turned in pursuit. His giggles grew shriller. They seemed to have played this game before. Matt ran to the corner of the living room, thrust his body forward and gleefully let out a stream of urine on the floor as he glanced back to check on his mother's approach.

"You little devil." She dropped the spatula and began to tiptoe. When she got close enough, she lunged at him. He darted under her arms and started leading her on a zig-zag chase, through the little house. "Eee-eee!" His squeals rose and faded as they ran from room to room.

As they ran around the living room, she

tripped over the spatula and fell to her hands and knees. Matt glanced back briefly and sensed his opportunity. He ran across the kitchen, pulled open the inner door and pushed his shoulder against the glass panel of the storm door. It swung open and he disappeared outside.

"Matt!" Nellie teetered to her feet. "Wait for me!" She stumbled across the kitchen, not realizing the storm door was swinging back to close.

"Nellie, stop!" I rushed to hold her back, just as both her hands plunged through the glass. She screamed as jagged spears ripped up her sleeves, cutting into her flesh. Then, momentarily stunned, she hung suspended across the door frame, while shards of glass smashed around her feet.

I was just behind her when she began to faint, reeling backwards. Catching her, I was able to break her fall, but she was too heavy for me to hold. I had to ease her body to the floor. She landed half sitting, her legs sprawled apart, resting her back and head against the wall. Blood spurted through the torn sleeves of her robe.

I dashed to the kitchen and grabbed two cotton towels from the sink. My own hands were trembling as I inched the sleeves up her arm to expose the terrible gaping wounds. Always upset at the sight of cuts, I had to force myself to wind the cloths around them. Blood seeped through instantly but she hadn't cut an artery, and gradually the flow began to lessen.

"Nellie, you'll be all right." She nodded, her eyes half closed. "But I'll have to call an ambulance. You're going to need some stitches."

"Matt, she murmured. "Where's my son? Where's Matt?"

"I'll get him," I promised, terrified that he might have run down the street. "I'll get him, as soon as I call the hospital."

I was hanging up the phone when the front door flew open. Matt burst in, flushed and giggling. He peered back outside to see if his mother was pursuing him. Then he looked across the room to the kitchen and glanced at her crumpled form. At first he stared. Then his mouth dropped open and he began the high whine. Suddenly he fell to his knees, rocked forward, and began to bang the top of his head against the floor.

I wondered what he understood. Was he really aware that she was hurt or simply angry that their game was over? Did he think he was responsible for her accident, or was he merely scared by the blood?

"Matt." I knelt by his side. "Please don't hurt yourself." Again I felt the strangeness of not knowing if my words had any meaning. "Your mother will be all right. It's not your fault that she's hurt." He kept rocking and crying.

Luckily, the hospital was just a mile away. Within minutes I heard the ambulance's wail and then two white-suited attendants were pounding on the door. Both dashed toward Matt, as if he were the patient.

"This boy had seizures before?" The younger man stooped to look at Matt, who let out a piercing scream.

"No—no, he's upset, but he's all right. His mother's been cut . . ." I pointed toward Nellie, who was moaning softly, her eyes half closed.

She groaned as the attendants looked at her arms. Then she suddenly screamed out: "Oh no—don't! Don't touch me! It hurts too much!"

"There's a piece of glass in here pretty deep," one of the men said. "I can feel it. I'll go out and wheel up the stretcher."

"Oh no ya won't!" Suddenly Nellie struggled to get on her feet. "Nobody's carryin' me away in fronta my son," she yelled, "or none a them nosey neighbors either." With a sharp cry of pain, she sank to the floor.

"You're a tough one, you are." The gray-haired attendant shook his head in admiration. "Let's take her by the shoulders, Ed. This lady's entitled to walk if she wants."

One man on each side, they all but lifted Nellie across the room. She moved her legs as if she were walking, but her toes were scarcely touching the floor.

Matt screeched louder and banged his head more frantically as they took her out. "I'll be right back," I told him and followed the trio to the door of the ambulance. They boosted Nellie into the back and she eased herself onto the cot.

Lifting her head weakly, she pleaded with me. "Get Frankie," she whispered. "Tell Frankie t' come home quick for Matt."

"I will," I promised. "I will." But they closed the door and I wasn't sure she'd heard.

I rushed inside. Matt was kneeling straight up now, wailing as he pounded his temples with his fists. I knelt directly in front of him, taking each of his arms by the wrist and holding them tightly in my lap.

"I won't let you hurt yourself, Matt. Your mother will be all right. The doctor will fix her and then she'll come home." I couldn't fathom his thoughts. His eyes were closed, his face contorted as he let out the steady high-pitched scream.

I stared at him, trying to imagine what was going on in his mind. Was there some primal bond between these two? The image of them clutching each other like monkeys the first time I saw them flashed through my head. Did he need to feel pain because she did? Did he need to feel like her?

Or was it less complex? Was he punishing himself because she was hurt, or reacting to being left by her, to the noise and the strangers coming in? Obviously, I couldn't know. All I could do was act. I reached out to hug his quivering body and found myself pulled into his rocking motion. "Don't worry," I began to croon. "Don't worry. Mother will be all right."

Five minutes—perhaps even ten—I'm not sure how long I held him. Gradually his cry became an occasional whimper. The stiffness slowly left his body and I felt him relax in my arms. Finally when he'd been quiet awhile, I lifted him up and carried him to the couch. He curled in fetal position, lying still as I pulled the sheet up to his shoulders.

"I'll be right here," I patted his head. "I'm going to call your daddy."

But Frankie wasn't at the laundry. "He took the truck to Watertown to pick up some parts for a drier," the woman said. "He should be back by four."

I didn't know what to do with Matt. It was only twelve-fifteen. I wanted to go to the hospital to be with his mother but I couldn't take him there, nor could I think of anyone who would come and stay with him. As I watched him resting quietly, I decided to bring him home. Perhaps my children would watch him there.

"Sure, bring him over," Richie agreed when I called. "Ellie and I will be here."

I found Matt's shorts and shoes and struggled to dress him while I explained where we were going and who would take care of him. The ride itself was a nightmare. Slumped on the seat, he smashed his heels against the dashboard, then into the windshield and the window on the passenger side. I was afraid he'd break the glass and managed to yank off his shoes. Then I drove with one arm clutching him tightly.

Everytime we stopped at a traffic light, he became violent—writhing, kicking, screaming. I began to slow down well before the intersections to keep the car rolling slowly until each light turned green. I talked to him all the time—glad that no one else could hear my monologue, aware that I was babbling to a child who probably wasn't listening. But I couldn't be sure what he might be absorbing, so I felt it important to keep trying to communicate. Matt in turn had only his actions—not words—to convey his fear.

I was surprised that I didn't have to carry him out of the car to my house. He cried but let me lead him by the hand.

"Is this Matt?" Richie asked, opening the door as we stepped on the porch. Matt suddenly leaped into my arms, wrapping his legs around my hips, clenching my neck in his grasp. We both almost toppled before I caught my balance.

"Well, I guess it is." Startled, Richie backed away. I carried Matt in, unclasped his arms and legs and slowly eased him into a chair, explaining again where we were.

"Richie, I won't leave until he settles down. But if he does, will you watch him while I go to see his mother?"

"Okay, Mom, but what am I supposed to do with him?"

"What's that noise?" Ellie appeared in the doorway, dragging the vacuum cleaner from the dining room. "And who's that kid?" She yelled over Matt's shrieks and the hum of the motor. Suddenly Matt stopped crying, and sat still, rubbing his eyes. Blinking, he stared at the noisy machine. Then he smiled faintly and, rocking himself, he nodded rhythmically as he kept his eyes on the machine.

"Well I guess he's not too hard to entertain," Richie smiled.

"Who or what's making all that racket?" Billy called downstairs. "I'm trying to get some work done!"

"Bye now, kids, and thanks." I smiled and started out. "I'll let you explain to Billy. Matt, I'm going to see when your mother can come home. I'll be back very soon."

"You'll find Mrs. Barringer in cubicle five," said the nurse in the emergency room when I got there. I pulled back the canvas curtain.

"Hey, Craigie—" she looked over as if she'd expected me. "Would you tell this here nursie my ticker's really okay? I been tryin' t' tell her myself, but she don't believe a person at all. She says they hafta do them tests."

"Now I told you, dear," the gray-haired nurse smiled sweetly, "one piece of glass is deeply embedded in your arm. You're going to have some anesthesia so the doctor can get it out. That's why we need to check your heart."

"Now lissen, sister!" said Nellie. Lying flat, she waved her bandaged arms. "Ya don't have t' be so snippy with them answers. Ya oughta be a little more respectful, see."

"The doctor will explain it to you, dear . . ." the nurse began to leave.

But Nellie didn't wait until she was gone. "That's what I hate about this hospital," she said. "Everyone's so snotty here—the kind a people who brag about havin' money in a Christmas Club at the bank."

"Someone bragged about that?"

"They don't really hafta say it—they all just act like they do. You know what I mean, don'tcha, Miss Craig? Real snotty-like. An' even when she wasn't actin' snotty, that nurse still made me feel real bad. All the while they was workin' on my arms she kept askin' me was I okay. 'Course I was! What a question! My arms was numb from them shots. But she made me feel like a baby. I woulda been better off without her. Ya' know how it gets ya scared, don'tcha, when someone talks real nice?"

"You ready?" A smooth-faced Korean doctor pulled the curtain aside. "Must be sure about heart before operation. Even little operation. You ready now?"

"Lissen, doc, just do your stinkin' test and get it over. I ain't gonna lie here all day long. I gotta get home. I gotta son, see, an' my son ain't like other kids. You can ask Miss Craig here—if ya don't believe me. Ain't that right, Miss Craig? She knows my son, an' she knows he's my main concern.

"Now I been tryin' t' tell that nursie of yours

I ain't never had no heart attack or nothin', but she don't lissen t' nobody at all. So just do your stinkin' little test and your nasty little operation so I can go home t' my son." Then she turned to me with a sudden look of panic. "Did Frankie get home, Miss Craig? Who's with Matt? Is Frankie with Matt right now?"

The doctor began wrapping the blood pressure cuff around her arm. I answered very slowly, hoping to keep her still while he checked her out.

"Okay. Everything fine." He wound up the equipment. "We take glass out soon. Very deep. So you go to sleep a little while. You wake up pretty soon. Maybe one hour, okay?"

"I tole you my ticker was fine!" she railed.

"Good luck, Nellie." I touched her hand as two attendants came in to wheel her out.

"I ain't scared. I just gotta get home real soon . . ."

I couldn't pay attention to the magazines in the waiting room and found myself wandering into the tiny candlelit chapel at the far end of the hall. "Please help them take care of her." I smiled at the images in the stained glass window . . . "But don't let anyone act too nice."

It was an hour-and-a-half before the nurse at the desk could give me any information on Nellie. "She'll be in the recovery room another hour or so. Then we're going to have to keep her overnight. She needed a blood transfusion, so the doctor wants to check her in the morning."

I bought some yellow daisies in the gift shop near the chapel and wrote a card telling her I'd stay with Matt until I got in touch with Frankie. One of the nurses would have to read her the message. After the cashier assured me that a volunteer would bring the flowers to her room, I called the laundry again from the phone inside the gift shop. Frankie still wasn't back. This time I left a message for him to call me at home. I walked through the lobby wondering how Nellie would react when they told her she'd have to stay overnight.

"The kid's a terror," Richie said the minute I stepped in the house.

"We'll never forget this one, Mom!" Ellie chimed in from the kitchen.

The house was quiet. "I don't see any terror." I looked around.

"First, come see what he did," Ellie said.

I stepped over the vacuum—still in the middle of the living room—and stopped abruptly at the kitchen door. "My God, what happened here?"

The contents of a shattered jar of golden-brown mustard had spewed across the floor. Orange juice from a smashed gallon bottle was flowing into the mustard. All this was dotted by about a dozen broken eggs. Ellie was trying valiantly to mop it up.

"The vacuum finally lost its charm," Richie said. "Matt came in the kitchen and started kicking on the refrigerator door, so I thought he must be hungry. I opened the refrigerator and before I could stop him, he threw out one thing after another.

"After I finally pulled him out of the refrigerator, he found some oven cleaner and started squirting that around. Man, that stuff's powerful! He had a fit when I took it away. But he grabbed for the window spray and that was safer, and it kept him quiet, which is why I let him have it."

"So where is he now?"

"In there." Richie pointed with his thumb. "Spraying the dining room walls with window spray. I'm sorry, Ma, but it's easier to clean than the oven stuff."

"Or mustard," Ellie muttered. "Or orange juice."

I found Matt—barefoot—in his shorts and rumpled undershirt, in the dining room, spraying Windex designs on the rose-colored dining room wall. He kept shaking his head, tossing the unruly red hair out of his eyes.

"What are you doing, Matt?"

My voice startled him. He looked at me—or rather just above my head with his maddening avoidance of eye contact. Yet he did speak, using our once familiar signal.

"Won?" he asked. "Doo? Dree?"

"Yes, sure, Matt—I remember all that: one-two-three—" And then I saw his designs weren't abstracts at all. He was spraying giant numbers, which were instantly distorted as the Windex trickled down the wall. He'd squirted the numbers one to ten along the wall and was starting again across the room.

"Richie—come look!" I called. "Matt's drawing numbers!"

"You weren't so happy when I used to write on walls!" Richie yelled back.

"But I remember what you wrote," Ellie teased. "You should have stuck to numbers."

"Wun?" Matt was jumping with excitement. "Doo? Dree?"

"Yes," I had to laugh. "Wun, doo, dree."

Flushed with pleasure, Matt began showing off—hopping as he moved around the room pointing to the numbers. "Wun" he giggled. "Doo? Dree?"

We all laughed.

"I read that Einstein didn't talk for years," Ellie said.

"So where's this genius?" Billy came downstairs holding his book. "Far out, kid!" He nodded at the walls, then stooped to be eye level with Matt. "Work in any other media besides Windex? Anything simple like pencil and paper?"

I expected Matt to scream at the sight of a stranger. Instead, he slowly reached his hand out to Billy's face, running his fingers over his mouth. Then he tilted his head and looked at Billy curiously. Finally, he uttered the first request I'd ever heard him make.

"Miwk?" he asked. "Miwk?"

"Well, I haven't got any on me." Billy pretended to check his pockets. "But if you come in the kitchen, I'll pour you a glass of milk."

"Don't let him near that refrigerator!" Ellie yelled. "I'm not washing the floor again."

"Too bad you don't know how to handle this boy," Billy said loftily. He lifted Matt onto a stool at the kitchen counter, poured the milk and—holding it aloft ceremoniously—delivered it with fancy foot-. steps.

"Here you are, sir," he bowed. "Enjoy your drink."

Matt grabbed the glass in both hands, raised it high and hurtled it to the floor.

"Woops!" Billy stared for a moment. "Could I have misunderstood your order? Didn't you ask for milk?"

Matt scrambled off the stool and ran back to the dining room.

"Tell me how to handle him," Ellie passed the mop to Billy, "after you wipe up the milk."

"I bet he wanted milk in his bottle." I said, picking up slivers of the glass. Billy started mopping the floor.

"Anyone want some tea?" Ellie filled the kettle.

"Not me. I'll watch the terror." Richie trailed after him.

"Oh no!" He returned in a minute, gagging, his hand covering his mouth. "I can't tell you what he's doing!"

I found Matt in the little bathroom off the dining room. He was kneeling in front of the toilet, lapping water out of the bowl.

"No, no, Matt!" Repulsed, I yanked him up forcefully and held his hands under the faucet.

"Miwk!" he cried as I patted his face with the towel. "Miwk!" he screeched.

"Shh-shh." I picked him up. "We'll get you milk."

I sat him on my lap in the living room chair and asked Ellie to pour a smaller glass of milk. Cradling him like a baby, I offered him a sip. He pushed the glass away from his mouth, stuck his fingers in the milk, and sucked on them. After he'd repeated this several times, he closed his eyes, resting his head against me. He whimpered a bit, then seemed to be falling asleep. I felt tired too, yet peaceful, holding him in my arms. Suddenly the phone rang, startling us both.

"I'm sorry, she's busy," I heard Richie say. But then he called me.

I transferred Matt to the couch and he began to cry.

"I think it's his father." Richie handed me the phone. "Frankie Barringer?"

I nodded and took a deep breath, preparing myself to tell him his wife was in the hospital. But he didn't give me a chance.

"Look, I got this here message where I work that I'm supposed t' call you at this number. Now I wanted t' check with my wife, t' see what's going on but she never answered the phone. Now that's unusual, 'cause she's never done that before." He paused, as if he too needed time to prepare. "So what's the story over there?" he asked brusquely.

I told him about Nellie and that Matt was at my home.

"I'll come right over. I'll take my son with me to the hospital."

"Would you rather have us meet you in front of the hospital?" I asked. "That would give you a chance to see your wife before you take Matt home." I wanted him to visit her alone but I was filled with apprehension when he accepted the offer, remembering Matt's atrocious behavior in the car.

Matt had stopped crying and was sitting up on the couch watching Billy strum on his guitar.

"There once was a boy," he sang, smiling at Matt.

"Whose name was Mat-tie." He plucked at a chord.

"How would you and your magic guitar feel about taking a ride with us, Billy?" I asked.

Billy's performance en route to the hospital was a great success. They sat together in the back seat, Matt whining every time Billy finished one song and paused to think of another. Finally he began a nonstop concert, filling the gaps with spontaneous lyrics.

"Now I am thinking—Mat-tie—" (chord) "Please let me think—" (more chords)

Mr. Barringer was waiting in front of the hospital when we arrived. Matt got frantic when he saw his father. "Bye now—by now—bye now." He rocked himself faster and faster against the seat.

"My wife would like t' see you," Mr. Barringer said, reaching in to lift Matt from my car. "Bye now," Matt shrieked. We watched him carry the thrashing child across the parking lot.

"Would you mind if I run in to see her?" I asked Billy.

"No, I could use a nap." He stretched his lean body out across the seat.

"Frankie was here," she said weakly as I tiptoed into the dimly lit room.

"I know." I stood close to her, frightened by how pale and small she looked, lying flat and still, her right arm encased in a plaster cast from wrist to shoulder.

" 'Fore he came I called my sister. I woke up alone, see, not knowin' where I was. Then my arms was startin' t' hurt." She glanced at the cast. "So that's how I remembered. An' then I saw I had this here telephone right near my bed. I couldn't get Frankie on it so I called my sister, t' tell her I was in the hospital.

"All she wants t' know, see, was did I wanna buy some more of them clothes her boyfriend stole from one a them Goodwill boxes. That's why it hurt, see, when they brought me in them daisies you bought me over there. It hurts when your friends is more concerned about how the hell you are than your own family."

"I'm sure she's concerned, Nellie. Maybe she doesn't know how to say it." I sat on the arm of the chair by her bed.

"Ha! Gloria can say whatever she wants!" Then she became very quiet. "But Frankie," she said softly, "he says, he says he don't know how t' tell me, but he's been real concerned."

"That must have been nice to hear."

"I can't get over it." Murmuring now, she closed her eyes. "Frankie—Frankie—he ain't never said nothin' like that . . ."

"I'm glad he told you."

But she was already asleep.

At ten the next morning, I called to ask her husband if he needed help with Matt and whether Nellie would be coming home that day. But Nellie herself answered the phone. "Oh, Miss Craig! I hope you ain't comin' for no tutorin' t'day, 'cause Matt ain't here. Frankie took him t' the laundry. He hadda, Miss Craig, 'cause Matt kept swattin' my arms all morning, exactly where I got cut.

"Then ya know what that little devil did? He went right in the bathroom and wrapped a whole roll of toilet paper all up an' down his arms—just like bandages. Ain't that somethin'—him wantin' t' wear bandages like me?" I wondered why she was home, but she didn't stop long enough for me to ask.

"Frankie tore it all offa Matt's arms before he

took him t' work, an' you shoulda heard the tizzy! Anyways, Frankie's drivin' a route t'day on accounta Matt, so Matt can stay in the truck. An' he's gonna take him out the rest a the week too, t' let me have a rest I mean. But—t' tell ya the truth," suddenly she sounded wistful, "it's awful lonesome bein' home without him.

"Frankie's gonna buy me a tank a fish—so I won't be so alone. He says it's a present 'cause I was so brave. 'Bout them cuts I mean. I'd enjoy it, honest. I'd like t' watch them little things swim around."

I finally got a word in. "I still don't know what you're doing home."

"See, after I seen you last night," she continued, "I woke up again real late, and it was so dark I felt real scared. That's when I called up Frankie on that there phone t' tell him t' come an' get me right away. But he says people don't get outta the hospital in the middle a the night. Then he says Matt was doin' good so I should take it easy. But even though that's what Frankie tole me, I just couldn't rest so good.

"So just as soon as it got light, I called up a taxi, see. I spoke t' information, see, cause I hadda get the number. An' I tole the driver t' come an' pick me up real quick. I felt real dizzy-like gettin' outta bed, but I hadda get home t' my son."

"But Nellie," I was really puzzled, "how come the nurses let you go?"

"Well—they didn't exactly let me." She

sounded hesitant. "When the nurse out in the hall seen I was gettin' my clothes on, she says I couldn't leave. But I wasn't listenin' t' her. Then she got another one a them kinda doctors that has a accent when he talks. He musta been a for'ner, I guess. An' he says it's bad for my health for me t' be leavin' without them checkin' me out proper, like they're supposed to. So I tole him, 'Lissen doc, I got a son, see, an' my son ain't like other kids.' I says, 'Call Miss Craig if ya don't believe me. She'll tell ya. So either believe me or call her. 'Cause if ya won't let me outta here, I'm not tryin' t' be mean or nothin', I'll tear this place t' bits.'

"Then you know what he says?" she asked indignantly. "I shouldn't talk like that! That's what he says! So that's when I really tole him, 'How about the way you talk, doc? You oughta talk better than what you do. I can't stand people who can't talk American.' It was the truth, Miss Craig, so I hadda let him know.

"An' after that he didn't fight no more. He tole the nurse t' write out some paper that says the hospital ain't responsible if somethin' should go wrong. Now, ain't that stupid! I wouldn't a been in the hospital in the first place if somethin' didn't already go wrong.

"Then they made me sit down in one a them chairs with wheels—an' the nurse pushed it all the way outside to the door of the taxi. I kept yellin' at her that she oughta let me walk. That's what I mean about them treatin' ya like a baby. Ah—" she sighed. "They made me sick—makin' me feel so embarrassed.

"Anyway, hon, I won't see ya for awhile—cause my son ain't gonna be home for awhile. Frankie's gonna be takin' him t' work."

"I know you're trying to dictate," Sylvia said when the intercom buzzed, "but Mrs. Barringer is on line two, sounding pretty upset. She said something about not understanding a diaphragm. Do you think she might be pregnant?"

"Oh-oh," I switched to the second line.

"Lissen, hon, ya gotta help me," she yelled as soon as she'd heard the click. "Frankie never bought me them fish he promised, so t'day I called me a cab. 'Take me to a pet store,' I tole the driver. I brang the thirty bucks I been savin' up all year."

I listened intently, wondering how this could connect with diaphragms.

"Guess what? The tank I really liked cost exactly thirty bucks. The guy gave me them fish for free! But he give me one a them diaphragms that shows how t' put it t'gether, an'—an'—" She spoke hesitantly, then blurted out, "I can't read the stinkin' thing!

"Miss Craig, please," she begged. "I know you're busy, but please could ya' come an' help me fix the tank? The fish are gonna die in that little cardboard box!"

She called again Friday, three days after we'd set up the fish tank. "Member that black Molly I bought—the biggest one of all? Well, it was just floatin' on top of the water t'day, like it was dead, ya know. So while Frankie was shavin', I operated on it with a needle. Cut it open t' see what was wrong. An' Frankie comes in an' says I was cruel 'cause maybe that fish was alive. But I knew by its eyes it was dead.

"Then when Frankie left with Matt I threw the whole damn tankful down the toilet. I thought they was gonna be more company than what they was. Just swimmin' around in circles all day. They was borin', really. It makes a person dizzy t' watch 'em . . . Besides, who needs them fish? They was causin' arguments. Ya know what I mean?"

I resumed the tutoring in the middle of the following week, after a frantic message from Mr. Barringer that he'd lose his job if he had to take Matt with him another day.

Nellie's arms were healing well by the time I saw her again. I focused my first few visits on her, except for the half hour each morning when she became absorbed in a children's program, "Sesame Street", and I was free to turn to Matt, who had no interest in the television show.

Each day I led Matt around the kitchen counting and naming objects, while I could hear his mother in the living room repeating the consonant sound being heralded that day. "M-M-M," she'd say. "Man—mouse—money—" She'd work out the words that were flashing on the screen.

When I complimented her on the effort she was making to learn to read, she protested, "No really! I enjoy this kinda learnin'."

But as soon as the show was over, her lower lip protruded in a pout until I left her son for her. Matt, silent but attentive during his time with me, began to retaliate when his mother competed for my attention.

Nellie and I were talking after she'd finished watching the show when Matt sneaked up behind her chair. I heard a funny clicking sound. She was so engrossed in telling a story about her sister that she didn't turn around.

Then Matt stood up, gripping a clump of his mother's hair in his hand. She must have felt the pull, but still she didn't respond. Again the clicking sound, then shrill giggles from Matt. Finally he reached one arm around in front of her until his hand was close to her chest. "Click-click" again. Then I saw that Matt was holding her silver cigarette lighter—and trying to light it an inch or so below his mother's breast.

"Oh—tryin' t' burn my boobies!" She laughed, knocking the lighter from his hand. "That thing's been outa fluid a week." Screeching, he ran out to the kitchen, then returned naked, having shed everything but white socks. He circled her chair in a taunting manner reminiscent of their interplay the day she'd fallen through the glass.

"Come gimme a little kiss." She reached toward him. He stopped in front of her, then he held his penis and sprayed urine all over her lap.

"You devil, you little devil!" She screamed gleefully, and rose to pursue him around and around the room.

In those first days of working with Matt he never once repeated the words I'd hoped to teach him. "What's that?" I'd touch the chair, the table, and while I was holding his hand, we'd explore each part of the room. "What's that?" I'd ask again and again. "Window—yes—window." Then, holding his hand to the glass, "glass." Then, "curtain." "What's that?" I'd point. "Floor." And I'd pull him down to touch it.

Every day we expanded the tour. Into the cupboards: the pans, the forks, the spoons. But after a week of Matt's silence, I began to feel discouraged. He hadn't even spoken the few words he'd used in the past. I made cards of pictures I'd cut from magazines, but Matt still chose not to talk. Nor would he count, not even after me. I thought of the day he'd printed "jeopardy" on the blackboard. I bought a twelve-inch slate at the five-and-ten and brought it with me to his home, but the only use Matt made of it was to pop the chalk in his mouth. Sucking on it, he stared at me blankly as though I were a fool to imagine he'd ever written a word.

Finally I decided to shift from language development. I'd hoped that increasing his vocabulary would facilitate our work in other areas, but now that seemed unrealistic. I'd have to approach him a different way.

Teaching him to drink from a cup, and then

to use the toilet—socializing him—would be the focus now. In front of his mother, I offered him milk from a cup. He washed both hands in the milk, splashing it all over himself.

"No, no, Matt. Milk is to drink. It's not for play." I took it away, feeling foolish at my own explanation. With my encouragement, his mother offered it to him the second time, raising it gently to his lips. He smacked it out of her hands, spilling milk all over her blouse. As she stood over him, staring numbly at her empty hands he reached up and began to slap at her face. She put her hands on her cheeks but made no move to stop him.

"When Matt starts hitting you, Nellie, try standing behind him like this. Then catch his hands and hold him firmly until he's in control. That way he won't see you as his target. See, Matt, you're not allowed to hit your mother. I'll hold you till you're ready to stop." Within a few days he was swallowing milk from the cup. Heady with success, I decided we'd begin his toilet training on Monday.

But Monday was a golden October day, and I found myself wishing we were out exploring the yard rather than heading for the bathroom. I could hear his mother in the living room, mouthing the words beginning with "P" that were being presented on "Sesame Street." "Pat—p-pet—pot," she said hesitantly.

Suddenly Matt slipped his chunky hand from mine and ran to the kitchen window. Moving his fingers erratically down the glass, he traced the course of the spiraling autumn leaves winding their way to the ground.

"Whuz zat?" he tapped on the glass. "Whuz zat? Whuz zat?" his voice rose higher and higher. "Whuz zat?"

I was excited to hear him repeating the phrase I'd used with him. "They're leaves, Matt—those are the leaves falling from the trees." I put my arm around him and for a moment he looked me directly in the eye.

"Yeaves?" he whispered, touching his hand to my cheek. "Yeaves? Yeaves?"

"Yes, Matt, that's right—leaves! I know what we should do—let's go play in the leaves."

Hand in hand, we ran across the yard, Matt stooping to pick up bunches of leaves, then letting them fly from his hands. "Yeaves!" He began twirling around. "Yeaves!" he sang. "Yeaves, yeaves, yeaves."

I sat under the maple tree savoring the thought that Matt looked like any normal child caught in the wonder of autumn. As I watched him dance across the lawn, a small plane flew low over the houses on Burley Street.

"Whuz zat?" Suddenly he was screaming, hands clasped over his ears, his terror-stricken eyes darting in all directions. "Whuz zat?" He seemed unable to spot the plane or even to recognize where the sound had come from.

"Airplane," I ran to him, lifted his chin and pointed to the single-engine plane. Whimpering, he sank into a sitting position, then tugged at my slacks pulling me to the ground. As soon as I sat beside him he maneuvered himself onto my lap.

"Wok!" he demanded, tapping his index finger on my nose. "Wok! Wok!"

"How can I walk," I laughed, with you here on my lap?"

"Wok!" he growled angrily and began rocking himself in my arms.

"Oh, okay! I get it!" I cradled him tighter in my arms. "The noise of the plane made you scared, and now you want to rock."

"Mmm," he closed his eyes. His lips were curled in a sweet contented smile. "Wok Matt," he murmured. "Wok Matt." I'd never heard him say his name before. I held him closer. We rocked together on the damp grass while multicolored leaves swirled all around us.

Chapter 11

Cᴇɪʟ's call startled me. The Planning and Placement Team had met and decided that, although the new school was still being remodeled, they would open one class before the end of the month. Matt would be accepted immediately. Ceil asked me to set a date to bring Nellie and Matt to meet the teacher. If Matt's mother accepted his placement in this special program, our tutoring sessions might be over in less than two weeks.

I hadn't wanted to keep this up for long, yet stopping now seemed premature. He wasn't ready, and neither was his mother. When they'd been separated before, I'd been free to devote some time to her. This special class would meet four hours a day. What would she do all alone? They just weren't ready. Nor, perhaps, was I.

I made fruitless calls to the Big Sister program hoping someone there would be willing to work with a needy adult. "I know it's a strange request, but have you got a volunteer who could nurture a thirty-year-old woman?" They'd let me know, they promised, if such a person came in.

To help Matt make the transition, I arranged to use a workroom at the school he'd be attending. We'd have it to ourselves an hour a day. Eventually, we'd visit the class he was scheduled to join, hopefully stretching our visits from minutes to as long a time as he could tolerate.

I told Nellie the plan and explained that she would come with us at first, but that soon Matt would have to go without her. She took it well the day I told her—but when Monday came, I sounded the horn and waited in vain. No one came out of the house.

Finally, as I was about to go and get her, the front door burst open. Matt dashed out, his mother stepping hesitantly behind him. He ran around her in circles, butting against her stomach with his head while she tried to fend him off with her hands.

The closer they got to my car, the more violent he became: ramming her with his head, pushing both hands against her breasts, leaping to claw at her cheeks. Suddenly she burst into tears, covered her face with both hands and ran back to the house. I expected Matt to follow her, but he ran through the gate and jumped into the front seat of my car.

"Gwaa!—gwaa!" he demanded, rocking as if the motion would somehow start the car.

So he really did want to come. But he wanted to come alone. I understood. In fact, it was my wish, too, but I couldn't play a part in his abandonment of her. She'd have to come today or neither of them would. I carried him, kicking and screaming, into the house and found his mother in the living room crying into a pillow on the couch.

I lowered Matt to the couch beside her but she didn't look up from the pillow; and he, still screaming, began to pound his fists on his temples.

"I know it's hard—but it's a really good sign." I had to shout above his screams. "Matt feels ready to come alone. It means he's growing up."

"You—" she gasped into the pillow, "you want it too. You wanta t'-t'-take him for yourself 'cause—'cause you don't want me."

"In a way, that's true," I agreed.

Slowly, she raised her head and looked up at me suspiciously.

"It's true. You're right," I nodded. "I do want Matt to do things without you. You're two very separate people. You both need separate lives."

Matt stopped hitting his head. Slipping his thumb in his mouth, he turned to watch as each of us spoke.

His mother sat up straight, still sniffling, but more composed. "It—uh—it h-hurts me t'-t' see

m-my son actin' like he don't n-need me no more."
Tears slid down her cheeks.

"I know," I nodded. "I know." Suddenly I
thought of my daughter Ann, preparing herself for
a six-month trip to Africa. "It's hard to see our kids
grow up. We've all felt like you feel now, at times.
Wouldn't it be easier for parents if their children
just stayed babies? But we can't control what's
inside them—" I felt as if I were comforting myself
as well as Nellie "—their amazing drive to grow."

"So take him." She waved her hand to
dismiss us. "Take my son." Then she reached over
and turned on the television set. "I'll be watchin'
my show." She sat with her head held high and the
volume turned up on "Sesame Street."

"No, I can't. Tomorrow I will. Today I can't
take him without you. I need you to come and look
at the school, and Matt needs you to let him know
you think it's a safe place for him to be. Tomorrow
I'll take him alone."

A sly smile played at the corners of her
mouth. "It makes sense in a way—" She snapped
off the TV set and grabbed her blue jeans jacket
from a hook in the closet "—you wantin' my son to
yourself. But at first, I gotta admit," Nellie glanced
at me fleetingly, "it made me feel quite offensive."

At first Nellie thought the new school looked
beautiful, as indeed it did. The gracious brick building was set in a grove of pine trees, a few hundred
yards from a placid lake. The interior of the former

convent was still being remodeled. The classrooms downstairs were ready, but the bathrooms weren't completed in the second floor children's dormitory.

Matt ignored the lake, the swings, the lovely trees, to become deeply involved with the hinges on the classroom door, the turntable of the record player, the casters under a movable blackboard. Each time his mother tried to transfer him from one of these spots, he'd beat on his temple with his fist until another inanimate object caught his attention. Then he'd begin again to examine it minutely. By the time we were leaving, Nellie was exhausted and much less positive about the school.

"I've got mixed doubts about this place now. Me an' Frankie don't care what it looks like. That ocean—can my son get in it? What if he falls in that ocean?"

I showed her where workmen had already erected part of the high chain link fence which would separate the yard from the lake.

"Even if he's safe while he's there," she said on the way home, "what if my son should miss me too much?"

It wasn't Matt, the next day, who acted concerned about the separation. "Gwaa! Gwaa!" He'd leaped into the car again and had begun rocking himself. Nellie stood waving in the middle of the street. I watched her figure diminish in the rear view mirror and felt I'd deserted a lonely child.

I talked to Matt as we drove, trying to remind him we were going to the place he'd seen the day before. When we arrived he looked bewildered, unsure of where he was. He started to walk with me, letting me hold his hand until we were almost at the door. Suddenly he collapsed to the sidewalk as if in a faint. Yet when I reached down to help him, he rolled on his back and kicked vehemently at my arms and face.

"Matt!" I called over his screams. "Are you going to walk or am I going to carry you?" The cries and kicking stopped abruptly. He wrapped his arms around his knees and rocked himself on his spine. "Carry you," he said softly and let me pick him up.

Somehow, symbolically, I wanted Matt to walk through that door, so I tried again what had once worked when he'd insisted on drinking from his bottle. I talked about how it was nice to play baby, slowly shifting to listing some of the things he could do now that he was growing up.

The frustrating part was that I'll never know whether it was what I said, my tone of voice or only some inner drive in Matt that made him change his mind. In any case, he did walk into the school.

That second day, and again the third, Matt was drawn by the brass hinges on the door, the tiny wheels under the teacher's desk, the way the toilet handle worked in the bathroom. It was as if he saw parts of things rather than the whole. Yet he could sit with me at a table for about a half hour and, when presented with one activity at a time, could focus on that task. I kept a notebook to jot down observations: "Matt can do primary puzzles with up to thirteen pieces. He can cut, although he does not always move the scissors well. He likes to paste, use glue and paint.

"After thirty minutes he gets restless. At times he seems overcome by some inner panic. He runs around the room, pointing to objects and screaming 'whuz zat?' as he works himself into a frenzy. Holding him or rocking with him in a chair calms him and seems to bring a sense of peace."

By the end of the week, quite by chance, Matt began what I eventually called his church game. I took him to visit the room where his class was to meet.

The nuns who once lived in the convent had used these rooms for Sunday school instruction. Someone had left a religious picture scotch-taped to the blackboard in the front of the class. It depicted Christ, head illuminated by a golden halo and his arms outstretched toward the little children who surrounded him.

Matt was attracted by it right away. Ignoring all the toys and furniture, he headed straight to the front of the room, pulled a little chair from the round table and positioned it a few feet in front of the picture. Then returning to tug on my arm, he led me to the chair.

"Dow!" He pointed to the seat. "Dow!" he commanded.

"Okay, Matt, I'll sit down."

He stood by the blackboard and picked up a ruler he found in the chalk tray. Tapping it against the picture of Christ, Matt began a long unintelligible sermon. Each time he punctuated his speech by hitting the picture with the ruler, he'd furrow his forehead and shout his garbled message with greater vehemence. All of a sudden, he put the ruler down and stood silently and sternly, his hands clasped in front of him. For a moment he even allowed his eyes to look into mine. I shrugged helplessly. I sensed that he expected something from me but I didn't know what it was.

"Gwaa!" Matt jabbed his index finger inches from my nose. "Gwaa!" he roared, his flushed face almost touching mine.

"Matt, I don't know what you mean."

"Ting!" he said angrily and began to wave the ruler like a conductor's baton. "Ting!"

Where had he seen a conductor and a choir? Did Nellie watch services on TV? Yes, I remembered her complaints about Sunday morning programs, that there was nothing to watch but "that holy stuff."

"Ting!" He rapped the ruler against the chalk tray.

"Jesus loves me," I sang, while Matt directed with the ruler.

"That I know—'Cause the Bible—tells me—"

"Berry good—" he interrupted and began another fierce, unintelligible sermon. Once again he stopped abruptly, rapped the ruler against the chalk tray and demanded that I "ting!"

This time he bowed his head and waited respectfully until I'd finished my song. Then he pulled out a second chair and sat close beside me. He folded his hands on his lap and gazed steadily at the picture of Christ. I assumed a similar pose but Matt threw a tantrum. He dropped to the floor on his knees, and pounded his forehead on the hard brown tiles.

"Matt, hurting yourself doesn't tell me what you want!" I took hold of his shoulders. "Please try to let me know with words."

But Matt didn't need words to convey his wishes. He jumped up and pulled on my wrist. He dragged me out of the chair to where he, as minister, had stood. Then he forced the ruler into my hand, rushed back to sit in his own chair and clasped his hands like a pious parishioner. So it was my turn to preach.

Matt had far less tolerance for my sermon than I'd had for his. I'd barely opened my mouth when he began yelling "Top! Top!—Ting!" And I realized my turn as preacher would be a high-speed version of his.

It didn't take long to see that Matt could persist in the church game endlessly. I was happy to hear him pretending to talk but concerned that he was locked into the repetition of the activity. His turn—my turn—his turn—my turn. I felt he might not stop unless I interrupted him.

I looked around, wondering how to do that, knowing how difficult transitions were for Matt—

even transitions from one activity to another. I knew there was a direct relationship between how close one stood to him and how well he received a message. The lower my voice and the closer we were to one another, the more chance my words seemed to have of being effective. And he was even more likely to tune in if I touched him as I spoke.

I put my hand on his shoulder. "You have a few more minutes, Matt, before we play another game." I had no idea of his sense of time, but the warning helped him disconnect from the church game. It lost its frantic pace.

"Pretty soon we'll be choosing something else." He began to look around the room.

"Okay." I touched his shoulder again, gently taking the ruler-baton from his hand. "Now what would you like to do?"

He wandered aimlessly around the room. Watching him, I felt sad that although he was almost seven, Matt didn't really know much about play. For a moment he paused, looking down at the blocks. I stooped down and began to build, stacking up three or four rectangles. "Look, Matt. You can make a house."

"No!" He swung his right leg back and kicked the blocks across the room. "No house!" Then, stretching his arms out straight, he began to spin, slowly at first. "No house—no house—no house—" He closed his eyes and twirled faster and faster. I watched him a moment, thinking of my first special ed class and a boy named Doug who had also chosen to spin.

"Antigravity activity," the consulting psychologist had called it. "One of the better clues in determining whether a child is schizophrenic. All children enjoy the dizzying sensation of spinning," he'd gone on to say, "but schizophrenic youngsters are apt to persist in this activity. As in so many situations, frequency and duration are the major clues."

Matt, like Doug, seemed to draw further into his inner world when he was spinning. It was a world I couldn't reach with words. Again, I tried to tune him into my presence by making physical contact. Although I approached him cautiously, laying my hands softly on his shoulders, I startled him. He jumped, his eyes darting fearfully around the room.

"There's nothing to be afraid of, Matt. I just don't want you to get too dizzy."

Matt looked confused. He shook his head as if that would clear his thoughts, then began blinking rapidly. Gradually he focused his gaze on the row of windows across the room.

"Yeaves," he whispered. "Yeaves, yeaves, yeaves."

"That's right, Matt. Pretty leaves."

"Pree yeaves," he repeated.

He was really developing a vocabulary. "Hey kid," I grinned, "you're getting pretty smart."

"Pree smart," he echoed.

"Okay!" I laughed. "Want to go out and see the leaves?"

But Matt suddenly began gathering up the blocks he'd kicked. He brought them back to the pile, lay down on the floor on his stomach and began to stack them together. I watched quietly. It was almost time to leave, but I wanted to see what he was doing. His building grew wider, taller, even more elaborate—empty spaces for windows, cylinders for towers, a ramp to every door. Matt was designing a detailed, complex castle—not the work of a retarded child. It made me want to forget his age—to focus only on the gains he was making: new words, interest in using some toys.

When only one triangular block was left, Matt tried to place it on the peak of the tallest turret. At first he balanced it perfectly; then with a fleeting smile he deliberately edged it off to the right. Both that block and all those under it cascaded to the floor. Growling, Matt threw himself on top of the rest of his building. Crushing it with his chest, he scattered the last few blocks with his flailing arms.

I wondered why he deliberately set himself up for this tantrum. Was he so used to frustration that it had become a source of satisfaction?

"Too bad, Matt. Too bad you had to wreck your building today. Maybe tomorrow you'll make another. As for now, it's just about time to go home. I'll count to three while you get up."

This time he didn't need my help. "Wun—

doo—dree!" he wailed. Then he leaped to his feet and ran out the door to my car.

The next few times I picked up Matt, he ran from his mother as soon as I arrived. Nellie, her shoulders slouched, would walk dejectedly back inside and watch us drive away. I could see her shadow through the living room curtain. I'll have to try harder, I thought, to find a volunteer for her.

Matt wouldn't wave to her or even glance toward the house. "Gwaa! Gwaa!" He'd rock against the seat until we'd turned the corner. "Bery good," he'd say and press his nose against the window on the door.

I listened to Matt with pleasure. His vocabulary would probably measure about eighteen months on a developmental scale; but it was increasing, and he was using words to convey his wishes. I knew that timing and motivation were probably more important than the fact that he was working with me, but, regardless of the reason, it made me feel good.

He'd even begun to use the bathroom at school. This momentous step proved so much simpler than I'd expected. I took him to the toilet and helped him undress. He immediately stood in front of the seat and squealed with pleasure as his urine hit the water. "Frankie? Heee-heee—Frankie?"

"Yup, you're just like Frankie."

I couldn't wait to tell Nellie how easy it would be.

"Look," she frowned. "What you do there,

that's a different envir'ment. Like Frankie tells me the laundry's a different envir'ment an' he's gotta act nice over there. It's just like that with Matt. That school place ain't the same as at home."

I poured out the whole story the next time I saw Leora for my supervision: Matt's easy transition to the new building; the progress, the disappointments, my doubts and uncertainties.

"Nobody really has all the answers on how to work with a child who has so many autistic traits." Leora turned in her swivel chair from her desk where she'd been taking notes, to face me more directly. "How could there be one method, when there's no consensus about what causes the condition?

"Every year I read that new projects will shed some light on the subject; on temporal lobe, cerebral spinal fluid, biochemistry, electrophysiology, genetic, biological factors in infancy—yet nothing has been definitive, so there's no specific cure. Think of Matt in terms of what we know already—he has severe problems in communication, behavior and learning. Then, continue to be yourself as you work with him. I think it's the best approach you can use.

"So far nothing, not behavior modification or anything else, has changed the long-term results. The brighter kids usually do well. The severely retarded ones do not."

I left her room thinking of all the parents in our area, all the parents across the country and around the world struggling for answers. I knew how desperate I would feel if my child were imprisoned behind a cluster of symptoms like Matt's. And if I thought that someone somewhere might be able to reach through, find the child inside and lead him out, I would never be able to stop searching and hoping.

I'd begun to think that labels like "autism" should be accompanied by descriptive adjectives—even ones as crude as "high autistic" or "low autistic"—so parents might have a more realistic idea of their child's future needs.

As for Matt, the diagnosis had never been clear. Autistic traits, cerebral dysfunction—the words no longer mattered to me. His moments of panic, his need to frustrate and hurt himself—as if banging his head provided some security and comfort—these were my concerns, regardless of label.

There were still those times, in the midst of play or taking a pleasant walk, when Matt's face would register nameless terror, as though a sweeping inner panic had overcome understanding. Sometimes he'd make bizarre gestures, flicking his fingers in front of his face, like an infant just discovering his hands. Yet I'd seen precisely the same movements practiced by bright young adults in mental hospitals, as if they were using hand signals to convey unspeakable distress.

I'd read of therapists using sign language for the deaf in attempts to reach nonverbal children.

This might have been a method to explore with Matt, but since his speech was already developing, I didn't want to start a new approach.

I wondered why his mother had never questioned Matt's strange behavior, but seemed rather to take pleasure in it at times. Most handicapped children had parents who strove to help them reach their full potential. Matt's family was so different.

Nellie's limited expectations were never clearer to me than when I was returning him home after a morning of tantrums. We found her waiting by the gate. "Ya know, ya oughta give my son a lotta credit," she said, as if she'd been reading my mind. "The sun was shinin' too hot out here while we was waitin' fer you t' come this mornin', so know what this kid done? Moved hisself right under that tree." She pointed. "Went right over there in the shade." She lifted him from the car and he burrowed his head in her shoulder.

Why, I asked myself driving away, have I let myself confuse my goals with hers? This boy, whose behavior would be so devastating for other parents, could please his mother simply by standing in the shade.

Although I'd continued to look for a volunteer who might keep Nellie company, I soon discovered my efforts were unnecessary. Nellie found herself a friend. Matt spotted them first, one day when we pulled up and Nellie and an old black woman were sitting outside on the steps. Shrieking, he ran from the car, pushed his way between his mother and the stranger and dashed into the house.

For once, Nellie didn't pursue him. Instead, she strolled casually across the yard, both hands in the pockets of her jeans, and leaned on the fence as she spoke.

"That ole woman's a blackie, see," she said as she pointed. The woman must have heard, but she didn't move, or look in our direction." Lives way down the road. But I seen her walkin' by most everyday, so t'day me an' her both smiled hello. She don't talk much more than that, so we been settin' kinda quiet, really. D'ya think I should have her in for coffee t'morrow? I mean, I know she's a old blackie, but t' be honest with ya I can't really make no other kinda friends.

"We both don't talk or nothin'. Just sit out there in the sun where it's warm. But she's very friendful, really. I didn't know anyone could be so friendful . . . Yup, t'morrow I think I'll invite her in for coffee."

The next morning I arrived as the woman, in felt bedroom slippers, elastic stockings and an old aqua raincoat, was slowly making her way toward Nellie's house. She was carrying a shopping bag that bulged with boxes.

From then on, as soon as Matt left, she and Nellie would put on the coffee and choose one of the paint-by-number art sets from the big paper bag. Her grandchildren, Nellie explained, gave them to her "so she could have a hobby."

They worked at the kitchen table, propping the illustrated box tops against the wall "t' see how the pictures are s'posed t' look when we're done." Together they filled in outlines of cats, dogs, horses, street scenes of Paris and even a numbered Mona Lisa. Nellie eagerly invited me to watch.

"Honest, Miss Craig, you oughta try it," she said. " 'Course you'd hafta buy a set of your own. I couldn't give ya none of my friend's t' do."

They both worked diligently, rubbing their brushes into the solid cubes of paint, carefully dabbing the colors onto the numbered boards. The old woman turned around to squint at me from time to time. She moved her lips, mumbled sounds I couldn't understand, then smiled apologetically and turned back to her work.

"She's tryin' t' talk t' ya, really," Nellie explained, taking a moment to wipe her brush on a well-stained rag. "She tries, but she can't always get out the words. Sometimes I think she's sorta like Matt, 'cause she can't tell people what she really wants. I think that's why he likes her now. He knows there's somethin' 'blocked' in her mind too." Matt had wandered in and stood beside the woman, his hand pressing on her cotton housedress. She put her free hand over his and patted him gently.

"Another way she's like Matt, too," Nellie

pointed toward them both with her brush "—they both get kinda fussy at times." She smiled at them indulgently, apparently not minding their attention to one another.

"She's usually nice," she continued as if the woman couldn't hear, "but she does get upset when she's irritable, like if her painting ain't goin' right. An' sometimes she talks . . ." Nellie paused to fill in a cloud with pink number fourteen, resting on top of a number seven purple mountain. "Yup." She stood back to compare her picture with the one on the box top. "Sometimes she can talk—when you're not around, I mean.

"Like yesterday she tole me there's somethin' wrong with one a her grandsons. So I ast her if she thought it was what you said one time—'bout how some kids ain't right accounta they got artism. I thought her grandson was one a those kids, but she don't seem t' think it's that. She seems t' think he's got a fear, more like Matt an' me."

The relationship grew deeper, although if Nellie knew her friend's name she never used it. "That ole blackie paints with me all the day now, till Frankie comes home at night." Frankie shopped for food on the way home from work, so the woman stayed as late as seven. Nellie thrived on her company. "An' Matt's doin' better too. He ain't runnin' around naked so much like he usta."

Nellie's confidence in her new friend was best proven the day I went to bring Matt and her to meet with Ceil Black and Matt's new teacher. Nellie got into my car alone.

"My son's stayin' home with my friend—the one who I paint with, that is. I don't want him with me actin' destructible while I'm talkin' t' that teacher. It might give her the wrong idea."

I was glad the teacher would have a chance to talk with Nellie alone. Since the Planning and Placement Team had officially accepted Matt for the school, he didn't have to be formally screened by the teacher. She'd get to know him as he and I began to visit her class.

After her announcement that Matt wasn't coming, Nellie and I rode part of the way in silence. She looked gloomy and sat as far from me as possible. I assumed she was either concerned about leaving Matt or about meeting the teacher. But she taught me once again not to make assumptions.

"It ain't this meetin' that's on my mind." She shifted in my direction, leaning her left arm on the back of the seat. "Just don't pay no attention t' me t'day." She sighed and was quiet. I waited several minutes before she spoke again. "It's somethin' else been makin' me mad. So mad it's been chokin' the talkin' part of my neck."

Another silence. She stretched her neck, moving her face close to mine as I was trying to drive through a busy intersection. "Don't ya wanna know what it is?" My nod unleashed a nonstop monologue.

"Ya know that guy I bought the fish from?—he thought he was *so* sexy! she said, mockingly. Well, yesterday I took a taxi down the pet store. 'Counta I still got the tank an' all. I tole him t' keep his stinkin' fish. I want some new pets now. An' I bought me two baby hamsters—fifteen bucks for both—t' put in my tank where them fish usta live.

"At first I was scared a them, really. But that guy at the store tole me they're gonna mate, an' I wanta watch them how they do it. But Frankie thinks both a them is girls. So I called that bum where I bought 'em an' I tole his ass off. I'm gonna do my tradin' elsewhere!"

When we turned into the long driveway leading up to the school, Nellie suddenly leaned toward me again, this time tugging on my sleeve.

"Hey, what am I supposed t' say when we get there?" Her eyes were really frightened. "Am I supposed t' say it's a nice day? What am I supposed t' say t' that teacher?"

Ceil and the teacher met us in the classroom. Four little chairs had been arranged around a low reading table for our conference. She slouched down in hers, eyes focused on the floor. But as soon as Ceil introduced her to the teacher, Nellie began to speak.

"By the talk of Miss Craig here," she didn't look up but used her thumb to point in my direction, "—by the talk of her, my son's been doin' very good. Learnin' his colors and numbers an' all that kinda stuff.

"But me, I'm real glad t' be workin' with new people. Now Miss Craig's been gettin' my son t' use the toilet over at this here new school. But I can't see discussin' how he oughta do the same things at home what he's supposed t' do at school. Like Frankie says, an' Frankie's my husband, ya know—like Frankie says, home is a different envir'ment."

Ceil smiled at me.

"I see." The teacher nodded sincerely. "Well, could your son . . ."

"Lissen—" it was Nellie's show and she wasn't sharing the spotlight. "Lissen, I miss my son when he's gone, see, an' I worry about him a lot. Now Frankie tole me all I have t' do is have willpower and get me somethin' t' keep me busy. Well, I got me a hobby t' do now an' Matt don't bother me so much. Just when he spits, or goes t' the bathroom on the floor."

The teacher looked frantically from me to Ceil.

"See, my hobby is paint-by-number." Squinting, she held out an imaginary brush as though she were dabbing paint on a canvas. "I do it with my friend—the one who's babysittin' my son right now. Actually, even though she's my only friend, she makes me sick in a way. Sometimes she scares me, 'cause she's always talkin' about dyin'.

"An' sometimes she gets a little nasty around the edges, about bein' black, I mean. Like she seen that TV show called 'Roots'—you know about how black people don't have none—at least in this country they don't. An' she started braggin' 'bout her grandmother bein' a slave. So I hadda tell her we don't have no slaves in our family, 'cause I'm just pure white, that's all."

The teacher, herself a young black, began to squirm. But Nellie didn't notice. Ceil, wide eyed, sat shaking her head.

"An' another thing that's not fair 'bout my friend. Frankie says he wanted t' take a paintin' down t' the stinkin' laundry, 'cause he says he's real proud I'm doin' art an' he wants t' show all them people. So he lines up all our pictures an' looks at every one we done, an' the one he chooses is one a hers. Course he didn't know that, 'cause I didn't tell him or nothin'. But he walks by real fast at every one a mine an' says the numbers is showin' through.

"At first it made me real discouraged, see. But now I decided t' keep on paintin' till Frankie chooses one a mine. That way I'll know if I'm gettin' good."

At last she raised her head and looked directly at the teacher. "So you can take my son. I can't really paint so good when he's around. At home when he starts that whinin', he gets in the habit a hurtin' hisself. See, he seems t' want his own way all the time.

"So honest, it looks like your class here's gonna help him more than what anybody's been doin' so far. I bet you'll teach him how t' talk. Conversation, I mean."

The teacher started to respond, but Nellie cut her off.

"Really, my son understands a lot more than what he thinks. An' no offense t' Miss Craig, or none a them doctors either. But no matter what anybody writes in them reports, Frankie—" her voice began to rise, "Frankie an' me, we want ya t' know"— her neck and face broke out again in those purple blotches— "my son, he's not retarded t' us!"

The plan was agreed upon. The following week, when Miss Harris started her class, Matt and I would visit. If that went well, Matt would join the other children. It sounded so simple, but I couldn't imagine Matt with other children. We rose from the uncomfortable little chairs and said goodbye. Nellie wooed the new teacher all the way to the door. "You're the first person t' come along that seems t' make any sense t' me, really."

"Well, thank you." The teacher was flattered.

"You know the definition of an expert," Ceil said under her breath. "Someone from out of town."

Nellie barely stepped from the room when she spat out her bitter condemnation of the teacher.

"That teacher's disgustin'! Did ya notice the way she sat, in that stinkin' little skirt she was wearin'? An' Christ, she got bigger boobies than me! Frankie would think she was really disgustin'. He'd never come t' no meetin' with her. That hussy's just lookin' for trouble!"

Out in the driveway she clutched my arm as her eyes searched mine. "Miss Craig," her face was creased with anxiety, "will this school be all right for Matt? You're my friend. I know you'd tell me, but it gets me scared inside. What if this school don't work? What if nothin' works fer my son?"

On Monday of the second week, Miss Harris moved in with her starting group of three. I led Matt to the window to watch them arrive, two boys and a girl.

Later, he kept working at a puzzle as I talked to him about their presence in the next room. At eleven, when I knew they'd be having their snack, I took Matt to look through the glass in the door. He stared and instantly began his high-pitched "anxiety hum." Looking is enough for today, I thought. "Okay, Matt, we can come back and see them again tomorrow."

"Gwaa! Gwaa!" He hit his forehead against the glass while frantically trying to turn the knob.

Miss Harris, who'd been watching, gave an affirmative nod to my questioning look. "Yes, please come in." She came to the door smiling warmly at Matt and telling the other children he and I would join them for a snack. But when she gestured to the empty chairs at the large, round table where they sat, Matt threw himself on the floor, kicking and screaming.

One of the other children, a thin dark-haired boy, pointed and laughed. The fair-haired one screwed up his face and cried in sympathy, or fear, I couldn't tell which. The third member of the group was a dainty girl in a ruffled jumper who nibbled on her cracker as if we didn't exist.

Matt, lying on his stomach, stopped screaming and raised his head just long enough to glance around. He spotted the smaller table he and I had used when we'd been there before. Crawling over to it, he pulled himself up by gripping onto a chair, then eased his body into the seat. Suddenly he began rattling the empty chair beside him. "Tit! Tit!" he demanded.

I sat next to him, and the teacher brought milk and crackers to us both. But he succeeded in pushing her away when she tried to place them on the table.

"Maybe tomorrow you'll feel like a treat." She took the food with her and went back to join her little group, speaking softly to them as they ate.

Very cautiously, Matt got up, tiptoed over to the bookshelves, and came back with a puzzle he'd done before. It was safe to do a puzzle—dangerous to eat or join the other children.

The towheaded boy kept turning around, holding his cracker out to Matt.

"That's kind of you, Bobby," his teacher remarked.

Matt ignored the boy even when he left his chair and began to approach us. But when he stood behind Matt, Matt suddenly threw the puzzle off the table, knocked over his chair and, jumping up, fled to the adjacent room.

Yet at exactly eleven the next day, Matt ran from our room and kicked on Miss Harris's door.

"That's not how you ask to get in," I said.

"Gwaa, gwaa," he pleaded, jumping from one foot to the other.

The group had just begun their snack. Again I wondered whether Matt had read the time—or whether he was responding to his own inner clock. We'd often worked with a toy clock, but he'd given no indication that it had any meaning for him.

This time he ran directly to the seat he'd chosen yesterday. The teacher calmly welcomed us both without rising from her place with the other children. But Bobby came directly to our table, both hands extended and filled with crackers.

"Cracker?" He grinned crookedly, stepping closer to Matt. "Cracker?"

Matt didn't turn but when Bobby was close enough to touch, Matt suddenly smacked the cookies from his hand. Bobby looked briefly puzzled, then smiled angelically.

Bobby sat on Matt's other side. Matt dashed to the bookcase, returning with his arms full of puzzles.

Bobby traveled back to the other table, returning to us with milk and a fistful of crackers.

Miss Harris, the dark-haired boy and I observed in silence. The little girl sipped her milk.

Matt, head bent over a puzzle, began a menacing growl.

Bobby broke open the waxed cardboard container and giggled as he dipped a cracker into the frosty milk. He sucked the soggy cracker and dipped again, each time laughing louder. Matt echoed Bobby's laugh. Soon the two were laughing together.

The next time Bobby dunked, he touched the cracker to Matt's lips. Spitting, flapping his hands, Matt ran screaming to our room.

But by Wednesday, the friendship was secured. Bobby dunked. Matt dunked. They both laughed and fed each other milk-soaked cookies.

I couldn't wait to tell his mother. "Guess what, Nellie, it looks as though Matt has found a friend!" But Nellie, looking downcast, had her mind on other things.

"'Member Miss Craig, I tole ya I got me them hamsters. Well yesterday, one a them stinkin' hamsters got outta the tank an' now it's lost in my house. An' the problem is, Frankie feels real bad about it. I could see the hurt in his face." She stared for a while out the window before she continued to speak.

"He never tole me, but he felt real attached t' them little things. An' I looked all over but I couldn't spot it. It hadn't even eaten when it ran away. That's why I feel so rotten inside, so guilty really. Actually, I couldn't even look at Frankie's face. I didn't know he cared so much for nobody."

Matt went back to Miss Harris's room eagerly on Thursday. But this time Bobby was having trouble. Gone the ingenuous smile. As he stood rocking himself back and forth from one foot to another, Bobby looked like an old man, his anguished face creased and distorted, his arms wrapped across his chest as though he were cold. "Where's Mommy?" he cried pitifully. "Where's Mommy?" he said as he rocked.

Matt would have had to pass Bobby to get to his chair. Instead he backed against the wall, his eyes darting wildly everywhere but toward the other child.

"Mommy will pick you up at noon," his teacher said comfortingly. The other two children, apparently used to Bobby's upsets, kept munching and drinking their cookies and milk.

"Mommy be right back! Mommy be right back!" Bobby's supplications turned to screams. As chance would have it, the distant wail of a siren suddenly came closer, then faded again. Bobby ran to the window. "You all right, Mommy?" he cried hysterically. "You all right?"

"You or ight?" Matt screamed. "You or ight?" Still flattened against the wall, he echoed Bobby's cry. Bobby heard Matt and turned away from the window. For a moment they just stood staring at each other. Neither boy uttered a sound.

Then Bobby began to smile feebly, rocking back and forth again, this time wringing his hands together.

"Mommy all right." His smile wavered. "Mommy be right back. She be right back."

Matt allowed himself to glance at Bobby. "Bery good," he said softly. Then, with his eyes lowered, he hurried to his favorite chair. "Bery good," he said again, as he began to work on a puzzle.

Chapter 12

W E'D agreed to try Matt in Miss Harris's class all day Friday. I'd talked to him about it, marking off days on the calendar, and felt quite sure that Matt had understood.

Friday morning, when he got into the car and hunched himself as far away from me as possible, I thought it was related to the plan and tried to reassure him.

But he walked into the building in the same dejected way and went right to the dollhouse in our little room. Reaching inside, he collected the family of miniature dolls, singled out the mother and lay her on her stomach, balanced precariously on the peak of the roof. Then he held the boy doll by the head, swinging it so the rubber feet knocked the mother off the roof.

Expressionless, his mouth ajar, eyes dark and blank, Matt behaved as though the action had nothing to do with him. After the mother's fall, the father was placed on the house, until he too was kicked off by the boy.

I knew Matt was showing me something that had deep meaning for him. As he replayed the scene, I talked about how angry the boy must be at mother and father and wondered aloud what had happened to make the boy feel that way. How I wished that Matt would answer. Instead, as though in a trance, he held out his arms and started to spin. I didn't want him to shut me out, to put distance between us by twirling.

"No, Matt." I caught his hand and held it. He stopped but wouldn't look up. I spoke about going to the other class, and like a robot he led the way to that room. Bobby, with no signs of yesterday's anxiety, ran to Matt and threw his arms around him. But Matt kept walking, and Bobby backed away, hurt and confused.

Matt went to the shelves full of puzzles and swept them all to the floor. Then he started banging his head on the side of the bookcase. The little girl instantly began to cry.

"You baby, you baby," the dark-haired boy shouted and pointed at Matt.

"You all right?" Bobby screamed, "You all right?" The room was chaotic.

"What's wrong?" Miss Harris nodded toward Matt.

"I don't know. If I can't calm him down, I'll take him out for awhile."

Choking and sobbing tearlessly, Matt looked over his shoulder until his gaze rested on the dollhouse, a larger version of the one in our room. Screaming, he ran to it, kicked at the walls, pounded his fists on the roof. When the side wall caved in and splintered with the force of his shoe, he began yelling "No house! No house!" and darted out the door, down the long dark hall. "No house! No house!" The cry faded.

I heard the creak of the heavy outside door as I rushed to catch him. He dashed across the lawn and found my car. He was banging his head against the door when I reached him.

"I'll let you in as soon as you stop," I said. He stopped immediately and scrambled into the car.

I was relieved to bring him home. Perhaps his mother would shed some light on this mysterious behavior. I was sure now that something had gone wrong at home, even though Nellie had said nothing about it when I'd picked Matt up earlier.

He sobbed all the way, his body shuddering convulsively. When we turned onto his street, he began screaming, pummeling the dashboard with the heels of his shoes.

"No, Matt! That's dangerous." But he wouldn't stop. I drove with one hand and tried to still him with the other. Nellie didn't expect us for hours, yet the door opened as soon as I'd parked, and out she ran across the yard.

"We came home early because Matt's upset . . ." I said as she opened the door on his side. He sprang from the seat into her arms, almost knocking her over.

"Did something happen here?" I leaned over, trying to catch her attention, but Matt was clawing her cheeks. He jounced and kicked in her arms as she ran with him into the house.

"Nellie, wait!" I followed. "I'd like to talk to you." The door slammed and the lock clicked. I knocked and called, but she didn't respond. All day I wondered what had happened to Nellie and Matt. I called off and on but she didn't answer the phone.

I got home from the clinic a little after six and knew from the books and luggage stacked in the hall that Bill had returned from his trip.

We stayed up talking until one. I'd just fallen asleep when the phone rang. I groped for it anxiously, wondering who would call so late.

"Miss—Miss Craig?" she sniffed "We—we been havin' a argument an'—an' now Frankie just walked out!" She burst into wracking sobs.

"Who's that?" Bill began to stir. "What's wrong?" I put my hand over the phone. "It's okay. Go back to sleep. Someone from the clinic is having a problem."

I waited a minute until her sobs subsided. "Listen, Nellie, I'm sure he'll come back . . ."

"Uh-uh," she sniffed. "Never! He says so hisself. An' he—he didn't leave us no money or nothin'."

"Nellie, there's nothing you or I can do tonight, and he'll probably be home in the morning. Now please, get some sleep."

"How can I—with Matt bangin' his head on the door where Frankie went out?"

"Nellie, I can't talk to you now. You'll have to call me in the morning." Bill was murmuring and I was angry at her intrusion, and at myself for getting so involved.

"What time?" she demanded.

"Not before nine." As I hung up, Bill reached over and turned on the lamp.

"El, dear—" He sounded so weary. "I was bothered about the time you put in on that case before I left. I can't believe she'd call you at such an ungodly hour." He sat up, propping his pillow against the wall. "I'm not trying to offend you by what I say." He reached for my hand. "But I want you to think it over. It isn't fair to us—to me or the kids. But what bothers me most," he turned off the light, "is that you're being so unfair to yourself."

I lay awake, his words ringing in my head. Nellie had taken advantage terribly. And I'd let her do it, thinking I had to secure the gains she'd made by being available to her. What gains?—I wondered now. Letting her son go to school? Finding a friend? Taking taxis to the store? Hardly accomplishments by anyone else's standards.

"Bill, from now on . . ." I had meant to say

that I thought he was right, but he was sound asleep.

She called at nine on the dot the next morning.

"The reason I called, ya see, is you was right. Frankie's gonna come home. He slept down the laundry all night an' me an' Matt was still lyin' on the couch this mornin' when he calls t' say he'll be comin' home. T'night I mean . . ."

I was not in the mood for a long conversation. "Nellie," I interrupted, "I don't want to take calls at home. If you want to make an appointment call the . . ."

"Lissen, that's the reason I called, ya see. Frankie does want a 'pointment for him an' me. He wants t' see who's right. In this argument, I mean."

The following Thursday at seven I waited for the Barringers, thinking with pleasure of the progress Matt had made. He'd spent the whole day in Miss Harris's class without me.

Several times I went to watch through the glass. He and Bobby did puzzles together, had snacks side by side, and played with the blocks. Once Matt looked up as I was watching, stared a moment and then waved hesitantly. I waved back and walked away. It was hard for me to say goodbye to him.

And now his parents were coming in, five days after their stormy fight. Yet Matt's improved behavior indicated that things were calmer at home. His mother had spent the days painting with her new-found friend. In fact, she was leaving Matt at home with the old woman while they kept their appointment tonight.

I felt anxious about the meeting—unable to get a sense of how it might go, or what I could do to prepare. I set up the room for counselling a couple—their chairs facing each other directly, mine off to one side.

Then the buzzer sounded, followed by footsteps on the stairs and Nellie suddenly bursting into the room.

"You sit over there, Frankie." She pointed to the seat on the side. "Me an' Miss Craig, we always sit in these chairs."

"We always have," I said, "but not tonight. Tonight I'm sitting over there."

They eyed each other uncomfortably as they settled into the two closer chairs. He was wearing his green uniform with the Manager patch on his chest. Nodding a greeting, he checked me out from head to toe in one swift glance.

"How it started, see," Nellie edged her chair a little closer to mine, "Frankie here's been comin' home earlier t' have his supper now, but my son don't like t' see him eatin' with me. So that's why he grabs Frankie's plate an' throws in on the floor. Then," she glared at her husband, "Frankie jumps up an' wants t' grab my kid."

"Ya know, hon," he tapped a cigarette on the arm of his chair, "I didn't really mean t' hurt ya. But when that kid spits at me while I'm tryin' t' eat my dinner, an' you just sit there like it ain't even happenin', I gotta admit it gets on my nerves."

"Lissen, Frankie," her hands closed into fists, "sometimes I think you're just too honest, see. Sure I admit Matt got some nasty habits. Like Frankie says, Miss Craig, he does spit when we're tryin' t' eat." She shrugged helplessly. "But that's no reason for him t' want t' bang that kid around. Now, me, I don't go for that—but Frankie here feels different.

"I think Frankie's got it in his mind he was raised rough, an' he don't get it that what I do with Matt an' what he got as a kid is two different things."

"Look—" His hands trembled as he lit the cigarette. "I *was* beaten, but we got smacked for nothin'. So, okay, I can't forget it . . ." His voice trailed off. There followed a long silence.

"I know what ya mean," Nellie had tears in her eyes when she finally spoke, " 'cause Calvin got beaten like that, too."

"Well never mind about me." He squirmed, then sat up taller.

"No." She brushed away the tears. "Ya know, Frankie, I think maybe you're right. I think Matt is just tryin' t' define you an' me. I mean, he don't obey nothin', an' I gotta admit that's true. But after he gets better, if we really help him, I mean, do ya think—do ya think we could maybe take him to a store t' get him some shoes that would just be fitted t' him?"

"Sure, hon, whenever he's ready."

I moved in quickly to support the idea of

their working together, while they were in a mood to cooperate. "So it's clear that you both want the same things for Matt," I said. "Let's try to work out some guidelines that might help from now on. I'll tell you what I know has worked with many children with problems." Nellie watched me suspiciously. Frankie blew smoke rings as he, too, listened with narrowed eyes.

"As a first step both parents must agree to be firm—but firm without physical punishment. That means if Matt hurts himself or has a tantrum, you both handle him the same way—by restraining him until he calms down. Whoever is holding him should also let him know you won't hurt him, or let him hurt himself. Let go as soon as he's ready. If he starts acting up again, go through the process until he's clearly got the idea.

"It means no hitting by his father, no feeling sorry for him and giving in from his mother. It won't work if he can play one of you against the other . . . So what do you think? Would you both be willing to try?"

Even as I spoke Nellie shook her head dubiously. "I dunno why, but I know it ain't gonna work."

Frankie, who'd been watching his smoke rings waft toward the ceiling, caught his wife's eye and sighed. "I'm the one who'd get it if I ever tried holdin' that kid. He'd scream and she'd say I'm killin' him."

"It sounds like you both feel helpless. If

that's true, Matt will sense it, and then you'd be right. Nothing would work."

"She's never let me do nothin' to discipline him." Frankie sank his face into both hands. "An' she's too lackin' to do it herself."

"Lissen, Frankie—" Nellie started to leap out of her seat. "You been downin' me too long! It hurts when ya call me lackin'. Maybe it's you ain't got all the answers either, like ya think." Her voice became shrill. "Maybe you're gettin' even for other things. You been mad at me a long, long time, and it ain't just over my son. That's not all you're mad at me for, an' you know that's true."

"Oh yeah? What else?" He looked up guardedly.

"I know what's goin' on with you, an' why you think I'm so lackin'."

His face began to get red. "That's not what I meant by lackin'."

"You been mad at me a long, long time, ever since I gave them stinkin' cats away."

"Course I was mad about that." He grinned and looked relieved. "But I kept it to myself, didn't I? But since ya brought it up, I thought you were cruel. I coulda had homes for all of them animals if only you'd just waited."

"Oh yeah? With who?" Jumping up, she wiggled her hips seductively. "Ya mean with them hussies that work in the laundry? Now what kinda homes is that? I'd rather give 'em to the animal shelter than that."

"There you go," and he waved his hand in disgust, "knockin' the people who work for me."

"Sure, sure," she said sarcastically. "You adorn everything them other workers do. You put all them other women up on a pedastone. All a them 'cept me. 'Cause you don't think I'm smart like them. Lissen, Miss Craig," she pleaded, "you don't know what it's like t' feel like you're nothin'. It's his attitude toward me that's very hurtful, really."

"Okay. Okay." He rubbed his palms together agitatedly. "If we're really here to talk, I'm going to tell the truth! You know damn well—" He leaped up and headed toward her, then glanced at me and caught himself. "You know damn well," his voice shook with rage as he backed into the chair, "why I got this attitude toward you. You know damn well why we're always fightin'! It's because you sleep with your son insteada me!"

The color drained from Nellie's face. She looked as stunned as though he'd slapped her. "Lissen, Frankie—" she whispered. "Lissen t' me. You got your nerve sayin' that in fronta Miss Craig. You got no lackin' in sex, ya know."

"Sure," he sneered, "sure! When you leave that kid for ten minutes to come sneakin' in my room—once a week or so—I got no lackin' in sex. Now what kinda life is that?"

I was stunned. Why had I never heard these sleeping arrangements before? Maybe she'd been

too frightened in the beginning for me to probe.
Then, I vaguely remembered the taxi driver who'd
told her that all we focused on was sex. But that
should have been a reminder, instead of putting me
off. Somehow I'd missed this vital information.
They continued to spar, unaware of my self-
castigation.

"You know it's not just the sleepin' with
Matt," he was saying in a subdued way. "It's the
feelin' I get that you want him all to yourself. Like
you're afraid you're gonna hafta share him."

"Just mind your own business 'bout me an'
my son!" She screamed, shaking her fist. "You
think a woman's supposed t' be like a light bulb,
just turnin' off an' on for a man. I ain't always free t'
go in your room! Sometimes my son would know if
I'm gone! Besides, by now, you oughta be used t'
sleepin' alone. You know he needs me more than
you." Panting, she waited till she'd regained some
composure, then turned toward me. "Ain't that
right, Miss Craig? I know you'll tell me honest."

"Nellie—" I was searching for a way to save
face for each of them. "It's really important for you
and Frankie to talk about your relationship, but my
real concern in this is for Matt. You've been showing him you want him to grow up, but sleeping in
his bed won't help him do that. Instead, it makes
him feel he's not ready to be alone—that he needs
his mother there to protect him at night. It would be
better for you and your husband, but especially for

Matt, to let him sleep alone. Just like you weaned him from the bottle, he needs to be weaned from your bed."

"Lissen, hussy, I don't need your advice 'bout where I oughta sleep, 'cause it's none a your affair." She glared at me. "This meetin's gettin' disgustin'. I ain't comin' back t' this stinkin' place no more!" She reached down to pick up her white plastic purse.

"Nobody's said one thing against Frankie." She pointed at him as she rose. "Like how he walked out on my son an' me. It's degradin', that's what it is, degradin'."

"I'll tell you what's degradin'." Frankie looked up at her coldly, each word emphasized with a jab of his cigarette. "Degradin' is living with you! Degradin' is waitin' for you to grow up! All your talk 'bout 'my son, my son.' When will you start actin' like a mother oughta?"

"You don't know nothin' about mothers, you creep!" Blotches on her face and neck broke out instantly. "At least my mother died when she left me! But you, you never had one! So don't you dare say nothin' 'bout mothers!"

"I know what a mother's supposed t' be," he spoke through clenched teeth, "an' it's the opposite of you. You're talkin' about mothers, huh? Get off it! You make me laugh. Giving up all your other kids to the state!"

For a moment I thought I had heard wrong.

Then Nellie went wild, and I knew it was true. Running over to where Frankie sat, she began banging her pocketbook on his head. "You said you'd never tell! You promised never to tell! You know that was a kangaroo court! You said so yourself. I didn't want t' give up my kids!" Crying now, she kept pummeling him, while he tried to cover his head with his arms.

"I never tole no one! You said you never would, too! I oughta kick your ass right out that stinkin' door!" she screamed, tears running down her cheeks. She swung her purse again and again. Cowering, he sank lower and lower in the chair. "First, you said it was a secret. Now you went shootin' your big mouth off! I hate you!"

"Now lissen, I've had enough!" Suddenly he jumped up, seized both her wrists and held them tightly. "Now lissen, I didn't mean to hurt you, but what's the sense of talkin' if we're not gonna talk the truth? You been feelin' bad about them kids for years, but we never say nothin' out loud. An' maybe that's why you tried t' keep Matt so close . . ."

She jutted her face close to his as if she expected a kiss, then spat directly between his eyes. "I hate you! I hate you both! You're both against me an' my son!" Wailing, she ran toward the stairs.

"That's not true, Nellie . . ." I started after her.

Frankie mopped the spit from his forehead with a wrinkled handkerchief, then leaped several steps at a time, catching up with his wife as she reached the landing.

"Listen, hon," he spun her around by the elbow. "We're gonna go home now and we're gonna talk about alla this. It's been affectin' our lives too long. I'm glad it finally came out. We're gonna talk and talk about them kids right now."

"Frankie—" She started to cry as he led her through the empty waiting room. "I-I—uh—I didn't think you was my friend anymore."

I watched them leave, his arm around her tightly. Then I went back to the office to dictate a summary of our meeting. I picked up the microphone, but I couldn't talk. My throat felt swollen shut.

Chapter 13

THE winter holidays brought many extra demands at the Center. The phones rang constantly with referrals about shoplifting, child abuse and suicide attempts by depressed adults whose loneliness was heightened by their fantasies of storybook family gatherings.

The six-year-old boy I'd been seeing burst into tears in my office after his mother's former boyfriend broke into their apartment, demanding that she sleep with him if she wanted money to buy Christmas toys for the kids. "Me an' my brother," he sobbed, "we both asked her 'please Mommy do it.'"

And there was the twelve-year-old daughter of a disturbed, abusive mother, who was being sent home from residential treatment for a holiday visit. Not wanting to go, she escaped from the bus on the way. The police had been looking for her for almost a week.

Our medical director asked everyone at the Center to leave their schedules open an hour each day for these emergencies. That's how I happened to have some free time on the cold, snowy day when Nellie called.

"I—uh—I know we ain't seen each other for awhile," she seemed to be crying, "b-but I h-hafta see ya now. Somethin' awful bad just happened."

"To Matt, Nellie? Or Frankie? Or you?"

"No, it's—uh—it's about my friend. But I'm callin' from the hospital, see. I hafta see ya soon."

Less than an hour later I watched her leave the taxi and trudge through the snow that already covered the sidewalk. She looked like a little girl, slacks tucked inside her brown plastic boots, head and body engulfed in a man's blue parka.

She hung the wet jacket on the doorknob in the office. Her reddish hair lay damp and matted against her cheeks. Her skin was paler than ever, her eyes tearful and swollen. Collapsing into the chair, she wept softly into her hands for several minutes before trying to speak.

"I—uh—I called ya from the hospital, see, cause I went there counta my friend." She kept her hands on her face, and I was having trouble making out the muffled words. "My friend," she gasped, "I hadn't seen her for a long, long time. Maybe a couple a weeks. Ever—ever since that time she— she took care a Matt when—when Frankie an' me came t' see ya.

"But th-then," she sniffed, "t'day after Matt got picked up for school I seen her grandson walkin' up the street. An', an' I went right up t' him, an', an' I says, 'Hey, what's happened t' ya grandma?' An' that's—that's when he tole me she was awful sick." Nellie stopped talking, wiped her eyes and blew her nose into a pink tissue. "He—he tole me they hadda put her in the hospital, in the part they call extensive care."

More composed now, she began glancing up as she spoke.

"So I went home an' called me a taxi, 'cause I knew she'd wanta see me. An' then I went out t' wait, an' that's when I met that stinkin' hussy—the one that lives down the road. Well she drives by an' sees me outside after I called the taxi, an' she pulls up an' asts me why was I cryin'. So I hadda tell her the truth, but then she says 'get in' an' she drove me right t' the hospital. Honest, the way that hussy sat in that car, I think she got them boils down there.

"It made me feel real bad takin' a ride from her 'cause I tried t' tell her once her rotten kid looked retarded t' me. But maybe she didn't hear me. Anyway I thanked her for the ride.

"When I found extensive care in the hospital, I seen a nurse at a desk, see, an' I ast about my friend. 'Oh she has hardery of the artery,' she says.

So that's why she couldn't talk so good. She was 'nemic too, but I think she said the 'nemic went away. But not the hardery of the artery.

"The nurse says it's all right for me t' go in an' see her even though extensive care is supposed t' be for the family. But, Miss Craig, my heart went out t' my friend when I seen her lyin' in that bed. Ya know them beds that has sides like a crib? Well, she was just lyin' there like a baby, an' her eyes was rollin' all around like she was lookin' for me.

"An' then," Nellie bowed her head and her voice grew softer, "I sat down and held her hand, an'—an' I tole her maybe it was true—I was a little jealous of her paintin' but I never meant t' competition her. An', then I—I tried t' tell her hers was the best, even though I'm paintin' better now than what I used to. But I wasn't doin' it good for spite an' I was gonna give the fanciest one t' her. My Lord's Last Supper—on velvet—it looks real nice.

"But her hands was so cold inside of mine an' she didn't say nothin' 'bout paintin'. She—she just sorta leans forward off the pillow," Nellie moved to the edge of the chair, "an' she puts up her arms like this an' she kinda yells, 'I'm comin' Jacob'—that was her husband's name—'I'm comin' Jacob, I'm comin'!' An' then—oh Miss Craig! My friend was gone! She was gone. I was right there— right there," she wept, "when—when my friend passed on."

"Nellie, I'm sorry."

"Why? Miss Craig, why?" She glanced up at

me, her eyes red and swollen. "Why did God hafta take my friend?"

I was wondering, too.

"Oh I know the answer, really." She began rubbing her eyelids with her fingertips. "I know He hasta take the people if they're always gonna be sick. I know He's got no choice, really, but Miss Craig—my friend—my friend." Sobbing, Nellie shuddered as she spoke. "I never thought she'd die!" Nellie bent over until her head touched her knees and cried and cried.

I stooped beside her chair and rested my hand on her back. Her whole body was wracked with grief. "Nellie, Nellie, you were a good friend. You made her last days happy."

"I—uh—I loved her." Nellie cried into her lap. "I loved her—but I never said it!"

"She knew," I said. "She knew."

We must have stayed in those positions ten or fifteen minutes. Nellie hunched over as she wept. Me trying to comfort her.

I looked out at the dime-sized snowflakes coursing, swirling by the windows and remembered Nellie's friend as she'd stood in her faded house-dress and worked at the paint-by-number board.

Suddenly Nellie sat upright and wiped her eyes with the sleeve of her black wool sweater. "Miss Craig!" Her frightened eyes searched mine. "It makes me think of somethin'. I could die, too! Ya don't hafta be old t' die! But—but I always 'spected t' see my other kids again—least one more time. What if I never do? What if somethin' happens t' me before I see them?"

"Where are your children now?" I moved back to my chair by the desk.

"See I never meant t' lie t' ya, but I didn't want ya t' know. That's why I ast ya once, when would Matt's baby teeth fall out. So ya wouldn't think I had other kids. I'm sorry I hadda tell them lies.

"I had four more kids, really, borned before Matt was born. First I had the boys, Charlton and Clark, named for them movie star men. They're about fourteen an' twelve, I guess.

"Then there's my girls. The two a them was twins, named Marilyn an' Sophia. I am still hopin' they'll be movie stars someday. But after my husband got killed in that dump, it got too hard t' take care a them all. I just couldn't do it no more." She picked at her nails. "See, before he died, I—I already got pregnant with Matt. An' I didn't want no one t' know, on accounta my husband an' me didn't live t'gether no more."

She glanced at me without raising her head. "I guess—I guess you think I musta been a hussy or somethin'. But honest, Miss Craig, one a my boyfriends—he said he'd marry me if I gave my other kids t' the state. Them kids wasn't eatin' good or nothin'. So t' tell the truth, I thought they'd be better off without me.

"But then I saw the looks my kids gave me when I seen them in the courtroom. The way they looked at me—I'll never forget it—kinda pleadin' like with their eyes. So I tole the judge I changed my mind. I didn't wanna give them away, but he looks at their records, and he says they hasta go.

"So the state put them all in foster homes, and the worker starts callin' tryin' t' arrange a reunion with me. She says the kids all wanted t' see me again, but I couldn't never get there counta I hadda stay home with Matt. See, I—I didn't want them t' take him too.

"An' then, the other boyfriend didn't want me at all. So thats why me an' Frankie moved out here. An' the worker didn't know where I was, so she couldn't call me no more. But it's different now. I wanna see my kids. They probably hate me now, but I know what I'm gonna do. I'm gonna call their worker an' ask her t' make a date.

"But would ya bring me? I can't go alone. You gotta promise you'll come." I promised—as much for myself as for her. What would the boys and girls she hadn't raised be like? Was Matt her only damaged child? I had to know.

"I'll let ya know." She began to put on her jacket. "I'll call ya after I talk t' the worker from the state." She usually rushed out when we were through. Today she lingered by the door.

"Miss Craig," she toyed with the knob, "about my friend that died t'day. I'll miss her real bad, ya know. It's a long day waitin' for Matt t' come home.

"But at least I'll still be seein' you." She

lingered in the doorway, as though something else was on her mind. "Miss Craig." She didn't look up. "I been thinkin'. I hope God realizes you still got a lot t' do. Helpin' me with my son, I mean. I hope—I hope He don't never take you."

"They only got one mother!" Nellie ranted into the phone. "I just called that stinkin' worker t' say I wanna see my kids, an' ya' know what she's got the nerve t' say? She says she hasta ask them other mothers how they'd feel 'bout that! Now what's she hafta ask them foster people for?

"So I says t' that hussy, I says, 'Lissen welfare worker, just don't be so snotty t' me, cause I'm helpin' t' pay your salary ya know. If there wasn't no people with troubles like me an' my kids, you workers would be outta business by now.' So she says she'll call me back next week t' tell me 'bout the 'pointment.

"I called up Frankie t' tell him I didn't let that hussy determinate me. Know what he says? He says I was growin' up."

When the social worker got back to her with a meeting date, Nellie turned it down and let me know in her own circuitous way.

"The reason I'm callin' ya, see, I got somethin' I wanna give ya for Christmas."

"Wait, Nellie—that's not necessary . . ."

"Lissen, hussy," she snapped, "don't tell me what t' do. I already wrapped your present. So what am I supposed t' do with it now? An' I done a lotta other shoppin' too. I got me that kinda spray t' make them holy pictures on the windows. An' I got me a cardboard Santa for the door.

"It's the first time we ever tried t' have Christmas, really. Frankie ast me who was I tryin' t' impress. Christmas is inside is what he says. But I think he's enjoyin' it too, t' tell the truth, cause he brought home a Christmas tree. The first one we ever had.

"An' that's why I can't go t' see my other kids. I got too much t' do right now. An' know what that worker says when I tole her? She says my kids would be disappointed, 'cause they was lookin' forward t' seein' me. Now I know that ain't true, 'cause I seen the way they looked at me in that court.

"So I says, 'Sure, you people lie all the time. So why not lie again?' Then she says I should call her back when I *really* wanta see them, like she doesn't believe that I do.

"So I called Frankie an' tole him, but then Frankie says it might leave scars if them kids was expectin' me an' I ain't got the time for them. But Frankie oughta know that Matt's my main concern. It's the first real Christmas he ever had, an' I'm tryin' t' make it right. Even though we ain't havin' turkey, an' I know that's s'posed t' be a holiday condition. But me an' Frankie likes pot roast better anyhow.

"So Frankie hurt me, really, sayin' I'd be

givin' them other kids them scars. Sometimes he tells too much 'bout how he feels. Honest, Miss Craig, sometimes I think he oughta lie a little. Like I showed him the present I got Matt for Christmas, but he says he tole me Matt ain't ready for it yet. I says, 'Lissen, Frankie, you're the one that tole me I oughta push that kid.'

"See I got my son the whole 'cyclopedia, every book in the set. Down the supermarket, they give ya the "A" free when ya buy five dollars worth a food. The rest a them books costs a dollar-forty-nine for every one. I just brought home the last one, "Z", I think. I thought Frankie would be real glad but he says I shouldn't a bought it yet.

"But, see, Frankie don't wanna understand that I just hafta guess, 'bout what Matt should get, I mean. I just hope someday I'll see the time when that kid asts for what he wants t' have. That would really be the pleasure for me.

"Anyway, there's so much extra stuff t' do, I can't be runnin' t' see them other kids right now. I tole that worker she'd hafta call again. I wouldn't turn them away, if they came knockin' at my door. But Matt's my main concern."

The staff always arranged a special lunch on December twenty-fourth: a toast to Hanukkah, Christmas and the New Year. Doug was telling a funny story about his son, when I heard Nellie's raucous voice in the hall.

"Ya know, it's disappointin' really." She was yelling to the receptionist when I went out. "We thought he was gonna enjoy it. But first he broke all the barbles off the Christmas tree. Then when he couldn't reach the angel at the top, he starts poundin' his head against the stinkin' door. It's a habit he got when he's mad.

"Oh, Craigie!" She turned when she saw me. "There ya are. Here, I brought ya a present." She handed me a gift-wrapped package about the size of our coffee table. "It's the best one I ever done. My Lord's Last Supper on velvet. Frankie says he likes it, too.

"But ya' know, Miss Craig, Christmas ain't what I expected, really. It's just as lonesome as the rest of the year. I guess we coulda had company, 'cause my sister calls up that she an' her boyfriend wants t' bring her kids t' see my tree. I woulda liked t' see my family, but Matt ain't ready yet. So I says, 'No you're not, cause me an' Frankie is takin' my son for a ride.'

"So she starts yellin' at me 'bout what's wrong with Matt. That me an' Frankie baby him too much. But I says, 'Lissen, Gloria, don't give me none a your advice. 'Cause you even tole me you smacked your son so hard he couldn't hear so good no more.'

"Anyway, I don't want no company till I get me a couch. My son's already ruined the one we got. But Frankie, he don't feel the same as me. So he asts this colored man from where he works over for a drink last night. An' that's why me an' Frankie had a fight.

"He says I'm prejudiced, but really I'm not. He says this generation's changin' in their feelin' about them people, an' a lotta them is proud a bein' black.

"But I says, 'Frankie, please don't let him come. It ain't that he's black. Me an' Matt ain't ready for no company here at night.' But Frankie brought him anyway an' me an' my son was so scared we had t' go t' bed at six o'clock. An' still we could hear them talkin' right through the walls in the room.

"An' then Frankie comes in when he left, an' he says he really enjoyed it, havin' a couple of beers with a friend. For the Christmas spirit, I mean. He says it's better talkin' to a stranger he works with than havin' my sister over t' the house.

"Know what I think it is, Miss Craig? For people like us, who been brought up by a lotta different people, like me an' Frankie was, it's better t' do your talkin' to outsiders. Even at Christmas. It just don't pay t' trust your family."

Christmas for me was gay and yet fragile. Bill was home for good, until he finished his book. Yet the family, I realized, would soon be separated again. Ann, having worked as a school aide, had enough money for her trip to Africa. Richard would be practice-teaching during his last college semester. Billy had decided to move to Boston with friends to try to earn a living in music. Even Ellie would be leaving soon to study art in northern Kentucky.

Watching the unwrapping of the sweaters, the sand-trek shoes for Ann, oil paints and music books, I thought of the airplane models and Barbie dolls that once littered our floor on this day.

Bill caught my look and put his arm around me. "We brought them up to find their own way." He drew me closer. "Let's be glad they're doing just that."

Holiday activities left me little time to think of Matt or Nellie, even though she'd called my home on New Year's Day. "We didn't mail no cards, but Frankie says we wish you an' your family all the best."

When school began again, Matt became so disruptive that his teacher called to describe his outburst of screaming, and how upsetting he was to the rest of the class. She mailed me her notes recording his actions on a typical morning, adding that she'd asked the Planning and Placement Team to consider putting Matt on a shortened day.

She had, she went on, tried to arrange home visits with his mother; but when she went to their house, Nellie refused to open the door. Matt, I felt, belonged in school for as long a period as possible. Yet, reading her notes, I understood his teacher's request.

9:15—Matt came in, put away his coat and lunchbox, and began to spin himself around.

9:30—The teacher tried to stop him but he spat at her each time she came near him. When she finally was able to hold him, he kicked her in the stomach.

9:45—The children were playing with blocks and toys, but Matt was uncontrollably screaming and crying. The teacher tried to interest him in painting, but he splashed the paint all over the easel and tried to run from the room.

10:00—He worked quietly on puzzles for about five minutes, then threw everything he could reach onto the floor.

10:15—The children were eating snacks while Matt ran around the room, whining and shrieking. Finally, he threw himself on the floor and began to pound his head . . .

I decided to visit the school to observe Matt and see if I could make any suggestions to help his teacher. I also called Nellie to set up weekly appointments with her. Nellie's intellectual limitations didn't diminish her emotional distress, and Matt, I felt sure, was reflecting tensions at home.

Months ago Dr. Diamond had suggested we terminate this case, but I'd felt then that I couldn't. Even now, there was still too much to be done.

When Nellie kept the next appointment, I told her about the teacher's request to shorten Matt's day.

"So my son spits at the teacher, huh?" she sneered.

"Well ain't that too bad? Ask her what color Kleenex she wants. I can see you an' her been havin' a sneaky little talk. Well it ain't my fault she can't control my son. She's supposed t' be a big girl now. Just tell her t' duck if he hits her. I don't wanna hear he's abruptin' that class.

"I'm sicka her complaints—her pushin' t' come t' my house t' talk. I ast her, 'Whatta we got t' talk about?' an' she tells me, 'Your son is botherin' them other kids.' Well, that hussy bothers me, too, but I haven't complained till now! My faith in that school is gone, I'll tell ya."

She jumped up. "I'll tell ya two things that's wrong with that place. One—" she pointed her index finger as she paced across the room. "My son came home with frostin' all over his face. Now the way I figger it, someone musta had a party. But I looked in his lunchbox, an' nobody sent me nothin'. I'd like t' tell them point-blank, they just don't care 'bout the mothers at all.

"Two—" She held up a second finger. "Yesterday my son come home without his hat. Now I don't want that hussy fallin' in love with my son. So she don't hafta keep his things. Ya' think there's trouble now? If I don't see that hat t'day, you might be readin' 'bout me in the paper. 'Cause I'm thinkin' a goin' over there t' whip that teacher's ass."

She sounded as though she meant it. "Hey Nellie," I said, "I'd hate to have you get yourself in trouble."

"Don't worry, Craigie." She sank back into her chair, and her face broke into an impish grin. "I wouldn't waste my hands."

Then I watched her expression change. She stopped talking and began to pick at her nails, but her mind was somewhere else. "Anyway, that teacher ain't all I got t' think about, ya know." She spoke as if to herself. "I got them other kids I ain't seen for a awful long, long time. "Frankie—Frankie thinks I'm wrong not t' see them. He thinks I might be hurtin' them bad." She began to bite at her middle fingernail.

"Why put it off, Nellie? You've worried about seeing them long enough; and when you're upset, it upsets Matt too. If you arrange the date, I'll plan to drive you."

"Okay," she whispered. "Okay." She stared into space. "I guess I oughta. I been dreamin' 'bout them kids every night."

The next day I walked into Matt's class just as he threw his milk carton across the room. One child screamed, another ran into the closet as the milk splattered.

Matt saw me but quickly turned away.

"May I take him out?" I asked his harried teacher, who was trying to quiet the rest of the class.

"Please," she murmured, rolling her eyes. "I'll call the custodian to mop up the milk."

Matt was pounding his temples with his fists when I reached down and took his hand. Startled, he looked up anxiously. "Hi, Matt," I smiled. His hand was trembling as his eyes searched mine. "Wun?" he asked hesitantly. "Doo?" His voice rose. "Dree?"

"That's right, Matt," I said softly. "That's what we used to say to each other. One—two—three. You remember, don't you? Listen, let's go to our room for a little while, the room where we used to play."

He walked with me as though he were in a stupor, but once there he was as destructive as he'd been in his own class. As soon as I released his hand he ran around wildly, kicking in the doll-house, throwing blocks across the room, jumping on the figures in the dollhouse family. When he'd flattened each member of the family of dolls, he put out his arms and began to spin.

"No, Matt." I caught his hand to stop him. "Spinning doesn't tell me what's wrong." He looked at me but his eyes were hooded and unfocused.

"I want to help you, Matt, and I know you're scared." He stretched his neck and spat at my face.

"No—" I shook his shoulder. "No spitting. No—no—no!"

Matt closed his eyes and began to whine, then suddenly dropped to the floor, his face buried in his arms as he cried. Good, I thought, wiping his spit off my chin. Good. I looked down at him. I hope you're feeling remorse.

He cried about five minutes, then slowly raised his head and looked around. "Wok?" he murmured, then sobbed again. "Wok? Wok?"

"Okay." I sat beside him. "We'll rock if you promise not to spit." He crawled over and climbed into my lap. Our bodies began to sway. At first Matt kept his eyes closed. Gradually, blinking, he looked directly into my face, moving his lips as if struggling to form a word.

"What is it, Matt? What are you trying to say?"

He inched his hand toward my face, then gently began to outline my features with his fingertips, exploring the contours of my mouth, my nose, my eyes. His own mouth kept moving, without uttering a sound.

"Tell me, tell me, Matt." I crooned as I rocked him. "What do you want to say?"

"C-C-Craig," he whispered, resting his hand on my cheek. "Craig, Craig, Craig."

Chapter 14

T HE Planning and Placement Team met to consider Matt's teacher's request to shorten his day. The group quickly divided—some agreeing to the cut, others insisting that residential placement was the only hope for the consistent training and handling Matt couldn't get at home.

The school's new consulting psychiatrist, Dr. Vogel, came to the meeting, read the records and suggested that Matt might be more testable now. He asked that that decision be deferred, however, until he'd met with Matt and his mother. With obvious relief, the committee accepted his suggestion. Ceil went right to a phone to set up a time for Nellie to see the doctor.

"Oh no ya don't!" Nellie raved. "Your doctor won't be seein' me or my son. 'Cause any a them people you pay is gonna side with the school."

"Tell them people over at the school," Nellie yelled through the phone the next day, "tell them me and Frankie's got a private doctor for my son. Frankie met him down the laundry, 'cause he saw the doctor's name on the package with his shirts.

"Frankie's smart like that, see, so he started talking to him right away."

"What's his name, Nellie," I asked. "Do you think he's a child psychiatrist?"

"Lissen, I dunno all that, but Frankie says he's honest. He tole Frankie right out, 'If I can't test your boy I'll tell ya the truth.'—So he's no liar, this doctor.

"So me an' Matt is goin' private. Frankie says we 'll pay that doctor seventy bucks. An' them people over at the school better never try t' talk t' him 'bout us, cause we're the ones that's payin', ya' know. The school don't get the report till he tells it t' me an' Frankie first.

"Myself, I think he's gonna help us more than anybody else . . ."

"I know, I know they've gone private," Ceil said when I called with Nellie's message. "And I just heard from the private doctor, asking what he's supposed to do about his bill.

"Now" she said provocatively, "for three chiliburgers, can you guess their doctor's name?

The one who has his shirts done at Frankie's laundry? Well, time is up; you lose. It's," she began to giggle, "it's Dr. Vogel!"

"I don't believe it!" I gasped.

"You'd better—because we've got a problem with it. He's the school's consultant—we really ought to pay the tab."

"Ceil, don't!" Suddenly I felt very serious. "If you do, those people will never listen. They've placed a value on his service—just because they're paying seventy bucks. It would be a mistake to undermine their involvement."

Later, I thought about my strong reaction. Punitive? Perhaps. But realistic, I was sure.

The state social worker mailed Nellie directions to a meeting place in Lakeville, about a forty-minute drive, the halfway point for the worker and for us.

"They says they'll meet us at twelve at the Family Diner." Nellie handed me the written directions. "Now don't that sound like a nice place for me t' see my kids?"

If I hadn't picked her up at home, I would hardly have recognized Nellie. Her auburn hair was pulled flat against her head, locked into a severe ponytail in back. Her pale, almost invisible eyebrows had been etched in brown pencil, her fair eyelashes drooped with beads of black mascara. Both cheeks had circles of rose-colored rouge, yet her lips were colorless and dry.

"Like it?" She caressed the fuzzy brown, fake fur coat she wore over black satin slacks. "Pretty fancy, huh? I finally got me a mink. My sister's boyfriend mailed it in a big cardboard box. Said I owed him twenty bucks. I says, 'Lissen, punk, I know ya stole it'—but anyway I sent him the dough. It's worth it, really. Frankie was mad when I ast him, but he didn't see how it looks.

"I started gettin' dressed soon as Matt got picked up for school. After I called that principal, I mean." Nellie filed her painted nails with an emery board while she talked.

"See, I says t' him, I says, 'Lissen, principal, don't try t' call me or send my son home early t'day, 'cause I ain't gonna be there'. He goes, 'Why not?' So I says, 'Cause I got other kids—that's why. An' I'm seein' them t'day. But lissen, it's a secret, so don't you go shootin' your big mouth off.'

"I'm really pretty nervous"—she bit off a hangnail—" 'cause I think they're all gonna hate me, ya know. The last time I seen them was in that court. They looked at me like it was all my fault. But they oughta remember," her voice grew angrier, "they oughta remember I tried t' change my mind."

Nellie talked constantly as I drove the country roads. How easy it is, I thought, to be enticed into her perspective of things. What she really means about her children is that she felt only fleeting remorse. Before and after the day in court, she hadn't wavered at all.

"I never tole ya' 'bout the time that worker

come t' our house t' pick them up. Before we was all in the court, I mean. She hadda chase them kids all over the place. The oldest boy, he was nine, he was sittin' in fronta the TV an' he says 'Take your hands off my brother, you motherfucker' t' her. They all was screamin' when she pushed them into her car."

God help them, I thought. I hope they've been in kind hands ever since. We drove past a vast lake, ringed with giant pine trees. I tried to focus on the beauty, to distract myself from Nellie's ugly, painful story.

"All I did," she went on, "was try t' ast that judge a simple question. I was never so 'amiliated in my life. I just ast him how come them social workers for the state is all such liars?

"I thought I had legal rights. Ya know, I didn't do nothin' outta the way. But that judge started yellin' if I ever say that again he'd lock me up. I felt real bad I wasn't allowed t' speak."

We came to the junction of route two-forty-eight and turned right, heading toward Lakeville. We passed large farmhouses and then clusters of tiny, closely set homes.

"Be watching, Nellie. The road downtown should be off to the right."

But she was rummaging through her purse for a match to light her cigarette. "Frankie says," she blew out a column of smoke, "it wasn't nothin' but a kangaroo court."

The road downtown was marked by a sign for "municipal parking." We passed a rundown drugstore with two pick-up trucks parked in front. I began searching for the Family Diner.

"If any judge ever says he'll lock me up again," Nellie looked out nervously, "Frankie says I oughta take my legal rights. 'Cause he'd take care a Matt. And I'd get out someday . . .'"

The Family Diner was a converted railroad car that had been painted red, with white wagon wheels flanking each side of the gray cement steps. A beige Plymouth sedan with STATE 401 on the license was parked in front. I pulled up directly behind it. "They must be here!"

"Frankie tole me," she interrupted, "just t' put my chin up high." Nellie's hand was shaking as she groped for the car door handle. "I tole him I'd try, but he don't know how it hurts."

We walked in silence to the entrance on the side. I held the heavy metal door for Nellie, who froze the instant she saw the group at the circular booth in the corner of the diner. All the other booths were empty.

"It'll be okay," I whispered. "Go ahead."

She cupped her hand to direct the words toward me, but her harsh voice carried clearly. 'D'ya think they'll recognize me? D'ya think they'll know I'm their mother?"

"Mother?" The taller blond boy rose, his light blue eyes studying Nellie's painted face. He looked awkward in the loose, ill-fitted sports jacket, his wrists dangling from the too-short sleeves. Yet I was impressed with his confident manner.

"Mother?" He put his right hand out. Slowly, tentatively, Nellie took it. "Remember me? And Marilyn and Sophia?"

He gestured to the twins, who looked about ten, sitting across from his chair. They were identical: shiny black ringlets framing rounded faces, deep brown almond-shaped eyes sparkling as they grinned up at Nellie.

"How are ya doin'?" Nellie didn't look at them. Her eyes were riveted on the hand her son still held. Their smiles faded as the girls exchanged anxious glances.

"And Clark?" The older boy nodded toward a short, chubby, curly-haired youngster with mischievous dark blue eyes.

"Hi ya, Ma," his wave was a kind of carefree salute.

Nellie didn't move until her son had dropped her hand. The three children slid closer to the serious young woman at the end of the booth, creating room for Nellie and me. Nellie slid next to her second son, and immediately focused her gaze on a plastic covered menu. "What'd youse all want t' eat?"

The younger boy stared at the social worker pleadingly, but she was looking toward me.

"I'm Eleanor Craig." I broke the charged silence. "I've been looking forward to meeting you all." The older boy returned my smile with a steady, appraising gaze. Clark's face broke into a wreathed grin. Both of the girls were intently watching their mother.

"Cynthia Brown." The social worker extended her hand. "I'm assigned to Marilyn and Sophia." I had to strain to hear her low voice. "But I picked them all up today."

I sat next to Nellie, the only available spot.

Nellie drew the menu so close it brushed the tip of her nose. "I didn't want that social worker t' park her ass with us." Her voice was low. She moved only the corner of her mouth, but I knew by their expressions they'd all heard every word. "I hope she don't write down no notes, 'cause that would make me nervous."

Cynthia Brown's voice was as flat and expressionless as her manner. "Why don't you children tell your mother how you're doing in school?"

"Awful, I hate it!" Sophia burst out.

"Me too," Marilyn echoed, jiggling in her seat.

"The only part I like is woodwork." Clark tried to look at Nellie, who kept herself concealed behind the menu. His eyes turned to me. "I just made a little stool, but I haven't shellacked it yet."

"I think I'll get me a pork chop," Nellie pointed to a pinkish slab of pork pictured beside gravy-coated mashed potatoes.

"I remember once you made spaghetti." Clark leaned toward his mother, his eyes begging her to return his gaze. Nellie abandoned the menu, eyes downcast, to fiddle with her fork.

"What else did ya cook us, Ma?" Watching her, he drummed the table top nervously. "I kinda forget."

"Youse kids was all fussy eaters." Nellie sounded annoyed. "How can I remember what I gave ya?"

The waitress came and jotted down the orders. Hamburgers and milkshakes for all the children. "Do you mind if I have french fries?" Charlton asked his mother.

"I hope your eyes ain't too big for your stomach." Nellie ordered herself the pork chop dinner. Cynthia Brown and I had tuna sandwiches and coffee.

When the waitress left there was another awkward silence, broken when Cynthia tried again to prompt the children. "Why not tell your mother about your other families?" She looked at the twins. "Your brother and sisters and other parents . . ."

"Lissen, you—" Half rising, Nellie leaned forward, jabbing the fork frighteningly close to the social worker's face. Cynthia covered her face with her hands. The children in the booth huddled close to one another.

Charlton reached out and pulled back his mother's arm.

"Lissen here, social worker—" Nellie sat down, dropping the fork on the table. "They only got one mother, see." She shook her fist at the trembling woman. "An' that one mother is me!" No one spoke as the waitress placed the food and drinks on the table.

"Now ain't that awful, Miss Craig?" Nellie

tore open three packs of sugar, stirring it all in her iced tea. "That's why I tole that judge them people is nothin' but liars." The social worker sighed and picked up her sandwich.

The girls begged a quarter from Nellie and played two raucous records. By the time the music stopped everyone had finished eating, intensifying the silence.

"Lookit the way them girls is sittin'." Nellie began to nudge me with her elbow. "Ain't they real ladies, Miss Craig? Wouldn't ya say they are? See how they're crossin' their legs 'stead a keepin' them open." The twins looked at each other and giggled. "Not like my sister's kids, shakin' their asses like tramps."

"Mommy—" Sophia basked in her mother's approval. The boys watched guardedly. "Mommy, Mommy—" She wriggled coquettishly. "Who do you live with now? Are you living all alone?"

Nellie shoved her empty plate away and wiped her mouth slowly with the paper napkin. "Well—" She looked at me anxiously. "Well, I wanta tell ya 'bout your brother, see . . ."

"Oh! We have another brother!" The girls bounced excitedly on the plastic cushion.

"Wh-what's his name?" Clark bit his lower lip.

"Well, where's the boy-wonder now?" Charlton stared at her with narrowed eyes. "How come you didn't bring him?"

"I couldn't, that's why. He's got a lotta

problems. Miss Craig can tell ya that's the truth. His name is Matt. That's all youse gotta know for now.

"Lissen," her tone became suddenly cheery, "I'm givin' each one a ya a buck t' go shoppin' cause I couldn't send ya no presents at Christmas. I didn't know what ya all like."

I thought immediately of Nellie sending the custodian at Matt's school five dollars for Christmas— "so he won't be rotten t' my son." I was stunned at her values. A dollar each for the kids she hadn't seen in years. She was holding her pale blue wallet, studded with a rhinestone poodle.

"Ladies first." She handed each girl a dollar bill, glancing briefly at her daughters.

"Hey, what d' youse two say t' mommy?" she demanded.

"Thank you."

"Thank you, Mommy."

Obviously pleased, Nellie turned to her oldest son.

"Thanks," Charlton said flatly, stuffing the money in a pocket of his pants.

Clark now averted his eyes as his mother handed him the dollar.

"We could walk to the five-and-ten. It's just a block away." The social worker stood up. "The children don't have to leave for another half an hour."

The excited girls ran toward the door. Clark sidled closer to his older brother. "Why should we thank her?" he muttered. "She's our mother. She's supposed t' give us things."

"Lissen—" Nellie looked up from stuffing her wallet back in her purse. "You're a little smart-ass, Clark." But the two boys had hurried out to the sidewalk.

We had to cross a small wooden bridge to reach the cluster of run-down stores that included the five-and-ten. The girls stopped on the bridge to drop pebbles into the rushing stream.

"Hey, look," Clark pointed, "up there the water's red!" A pipe from the clothing factory next to the bridge was spurting red dye into the stream. "Our teacher says they're not supposed to do that."

"Yeah?" Looking amused, Charlton leaned his elbow on the rail of the bridge. "Well, people aren't supposed to give kids away either, but look what happened to us. You're my brother, but I haven't seen you for a couple of years."

"How far apart do you two live?" Nellie was walking ahead with the girls. I was glad for the chance to talk to her sons.

The boys, too, wanted to talk. Both began pouring out stories of their experiences in various foster homes. Charlton had been in only two, but Clark had been moved five times.

"The worker says it's not my fault. But they woulda kept me if they really liked me." He was happy now, he said—his fourth month with a policeman, his wife and two sons. "But Tommy tries to get me in trouble 'cause he doesn't like to share his room. When I grow up I want a house with a hundred rooms, for all the kids that no one wants."

We talked until we reached the store. The merchandise displayed in the window was covered with dust.

"Oh boy," Charlton exclaimed, "they've got a record sale." Both he and Clark dashed in, close behind Nellie and her daughters.

Cynthia, who'd trailed along, now stood on the sidewalk with me. "The sun feels good," she remarked. "When we started out, I was afraid it was going to snow."

I looked at Cynthia, wondering why someone so apathetic would take such a demanding job. She wore no makeup on her waxy-yellow skin. There were dark circles under her brown eyes and deep lines carved in her cheeks. Her brown hair was long, but sparse and thin. Like her personality, it lacked tone and vitality. She could have been any age, I thought, from thirty to forty-five.

"I wanted to ask you about her other son . . . " I found her voice flat and grating.

"We don't have definitive answers." I didn't want to talk about Matt. "Nellie's right when she says he has problems. There'll be some testing soon, which we hope will be revealing. If she'll sign a release, we can send you a copy."

"Okay," she nodded, using her hand as a visor to keep the sun from her eyes.

"I've been wondering," I said, "what you could tell me about these children."

"What couldn't I tell!" she sighed. "Let's sit

down a few minutes." We moved to the slatted green bench at the bus stop next to the five-and-ten.

"This family," she sighed, "certainly isn't new to us. To tell you the truth, it's sort of a test case in our office. Their name came up so often our supervisor asked me to do a family study, a kind of a family tree, from Nellie Barringer's two sets of grandparents—the Applebys and the Troys—right to the newest infant."

Facing me on the bench, Cynthia Brown looked different. Her features reflected an involvement and intensity she hadn't shown before.

"Everyone at the office was stunned by what we found. Beginning with maternal and paternal grandparents, there are more than one hundred people in this family either on welfare or in foster-care. Right now one of her aunts is at Long Meadow, the state mental hospital; two uncles and a brother are in jail. Both sets of grandparents were alcoholics. All the siblings have been arrested at one time or another as petty thieves. One of her older nephews is being held for rape."

My mind was reeling with this information. I tried to sort it out in terms of Matt.

"Like Mrs. Barringer," she went on, "the girls in the family start spewing out children at the age of thirteen, but their relationships with men seldom last more than a year or two and often end in brutality. Last year one of the fifteen-year-old girls was stabbed to death by a thirty-year-old boyfriend. Her two children were put in foster-care together, but the three-year-old threw the baby out of his crib and the infant's still in a coma.

"These are some of the ugly details. You can imagine how disturbed all the children become. By ten, they're ready to inflict their pain on the world without any scruples. One generation after another gets trapped in this self-perpetuating cycle."

"What about these kids?" I asked.

"Relatively lucky," she nodded. "They've got more of a chance, being raised in foster homes. At least they see role-models with different values. But of course they've also been damaged by Mrs. Barringer's rejection of them, as well as by all the shuffling around. Some foster parents want to get out of their commitments when the going gets really rough. You know what that can do—what it's already done to their mother.

"Look, enough! I'm sorry!" She put up her hands to signal "stop." "I really get wound up about this. I just can't help it." Her face looked drawn again, as though she'd been burdened to the point of despair.

"Funny," she chuckled bitterly, "I remember a debate in our class on character development—how seriously we argued genetics versus environment. The old are-they-born-that-way-or-did-we-do-it-to-them dilemma.

"It looked simple until I took on this family. After I'd traced the genealogy, the supervisor asked me to present it to the rest of the staff. Life experience or poor genes—they all wanted my opinion." She stopped talking, and fingered the ring of keys she'd taken from her purse.

"Did you come to any conclusion?" I prompted softly.

"Conclusion? My conclusion was I should look for a better job—that's all. I'm twenty-eight but I look older than my mother. All I know is that the longer I stay with Protective Service, the more discouraged I get: The case loads are overwhelming. The pay is lousy. No one wants to work there very long, so the turnover is enormous. Kids who are getting bounced from home to home are also getting different workers, too.

"But even these problems wouldn't be so hard to take if I thought that what we're doing was really effective. Oh, sometimes, maybe, it is. But in a family like this I don't know what would really change the patterns.

"I had to struggle to get the twins an hour of counselling a week. The boys don't even get that. The only time the other children in the family have gotten any help is after a crisis, when someone's hurt or goes to jail.

"Look, I'm sorry." She stood up. "I realize I've been making a speech. I guess I want you people in agencies to know we try as hard as possible. I know it's easy to criticize Protective Service. But think of the volume. More than one hundred in this family alone! In the long run who can save them all?"

Chapter 15

WE walked into the store together and looked around for Nellie and the children. I suspected she might be angry with me for having talked to Cynthia. But she and Marilyn were standing together at the counter under a sign that read CASHIER.

"I'm buying this for my mother." Marilyn held up a fancy floral handkerchief for Cynthia and me to see. "It's sixty-nine cents." Nellie beamed. The cashier handed the girl her purchase, now stapled in a brown paper bag.

"I'm gonna give it to her soon as I get in the house."

Nellie's face got hard and ugly. Her eyes

narrowed, her lips tightened. She grabbed the child, who began to wince.

"Lissen, you!" Nellie shook her shoulder. The child dropped the bag. Wiping her eyes, Marilyn stooped to retrieve it. The three other children stood staring at Nellie from their scattered positions in the almost deserted store.

"Lissen, you—" Nellie shook the child again as soon as she stood up. "An' that goes for all a youse, too—" She looked around at the others. "You only got one mother, I tole ya, an' that one mother is me!" The girl began to weep openly.

"I coulda had three hundred bucks a month," Nellie was relentless, "if I wanted t' keep all youse kids." I was shocked that anyone could be so vindictive.

"Then why didn't you?" Her second son screamed from his place in the record aisle. "Why didn't you keep us? I used to ask everyone where you were. I used to dream about you all the time. I thought I musta been real bad, for you t' give me away. I thought if I tried to be good you'd take me back. But, no!" His voice began to choke. "You had t' get another kid and start all over again. The hell with us!" he cried. "The hell with us!"

Clark collapsed on the counter, sobbing into his hands. His older brother went to him.

"Shh—it's okay, Clark." Charlton put a comforting arm around the distraught boy. "Shh. Don't bother trying to make her love you cause it won't work.

"C'mon," he led his brother out of the store. "C'mon. It's not our fault. It's her—not us—that's wrong." Nellie stared as her sons passed her by.

The boys had already crossed the bridge and were waiting beside Cynthia's car. The little girl to whom Nellie had been so cruel clutched her social worker's hand and walked morosely over the bridge.

Her sister, Sophia, skipped along beside me, chatting about school and the new baby in the family where she lived. Nellie walked ahead with swift purposeful strides, her jaw thrust out pugnaciously.

"Well," Cynthia shook my hand when we'd gathered by her car, "thanks for driving Mrs. Barringer." Her eyes met mine knowingly.

"Goodbye, Ma." Only Sophia stepped forward to kiss her mother. Nellie turned her face away from the child, who flushed as though she'd been slapped. Her sister grabbed her arm and pulled her back to the little circle her siblings had formed.

"I've got a question." Clark squinted in the sunlight. "I'm supposed to ask it for my social studies class. What nationality are we anyhow?" The four children stared at Nellie.

She barely moved her lips. "I think you all is English an' American."

"All set?" Making an effort to sound cheerful, Cynthia walked to the driver's side of the car.

"Almost." Charlton held up his hand. "We need another minute." Clark and his sisters crowded closer to him, as if they knew what he planned to say.

"We all want to know—" Charlton's glance encompassed the others, "we all want to know where our father is buried." All eyes were on Nellie's face.

"Now why d' ya wanta know a thing like that?" Nellie shot back huffily.

He hung his head, and the other children also bowed theirs. "So we could put some flowers on his grave."

"Lissen, the city buried him, an' I don't think they mark them city graves with nothin'."

Nellie looked the other way while the children got in the car and I returned their waves.

"The nerve a them kids," she headed toward my car. "How dumb can any kids get? Can't they just look at each other an' tell they all had different fathers? 'Cept them twins, a course. My husband who died—he was only the father of the biggest one."

I let her wait in the car while I stood behind it struggling with my feelings of rage. She had to be the coldest woman I'd ever met! Thank God they'd been taken from her. A tragedy that she'd successfully hidden Matt away, her morbid needs keeping him at an animal level of existence.

At least these four, all products of the same

womb as Matt, were free to lead reasonably normal lives in foster homes. Their opportunities would be limited, perhaps. But this disturbed woman would not inflict her pathology on them, as she'd done with her youngest son.

"I felt cold leavin' them kids," she said as I started the motor. "I feel cold 'bout them now. Matt—I love very much. It ain't the same feelin' when I saw them other kids. An' they all was cold t' me too. I tried t' love them all, but not one a them tried t' return it.

"Can you imagine that boy, askin' me why I didn't keep them? What if I ever let them girls come live with me? Pretty soon they'd be women, an' what if they started trouble with the neighbors? Sleepin' around with them men. I s'pose people would think that I'd be the one t' blame.

"No." She shook her head. "It never woulda worked. They spoiled my appetite really. I couldn't enjoy them pork chops.

"I'm buyin' this hanky for my mother." She mimicked her daughter. "Only it wasn't even for me! An' them boys had other brothers, too. They don't care nothin' bout Matt! Well, I don't think I wanta see them anymore." She wrapped herself tighter in her fake mink coat. "It ain't fair, when it's my turn t' see them, an' all they talk about is them other people."

"Those people are trying to give them what they need." I spoke quietly, but I felt like shouting.

I wanted to see whether she was capable of feeling some of the hurt she so readily inflicted on others. "You should be grateful that there are people willing to raise your kids!"

"Yeah?" She tapped her cigarette in the ashtray as I sped to get her home. "Maybe you think I oughta send them people a money order. It don't mean nothin' t' you that the state is payin' them three hundred bucks."

"Three hundred dollars a month for four children isn't enough, Nellie. The money doesn't cover their expenses." Nellie didn't answer at first, and then she changed her tactics.

"Ya know that oldest one, I think he acts pretty queer." She glanced at me as if gauging my reaction. "An' them twins, I think they oughta be gettin' some help. Them foster people don't seem t' notice, them girls is quite 'hyperactive.'"

Suddenly the image of Matt appeared in my mind, the day the serviceman had found him in the basement, his pallid skin flashing as the naked boy ran through the shadows to empty his bowels in a darkened corner. How ironic to hear her assess the other children's needs, their foster parents' shortcomings.

"Nellie, listen a minute, will you?"

"All right, all right Miss Craig. Jeez, ya don't hafta yell . . ."

"Your other children are doing well. Their foster parents must be trying very hard. I'm glad they're in good homes. Maybe you've kept Matt from growing up because the others were taken away. But you're not doing as well with him as those foster parents do with your other children!" I didn't care about her reaction. I was glad I'd said what I thought.

"Huh! How d' ya figger that?" She snickered. "Me not lettin' Matt grow up . . ."

"C'mon Nellie! You sleep with him. He goes to the bathroom on the floor. He eats like a dog. You could change all that if you really wanted to!"

She turned away from me to gaze out the window. "Lissen, Miss Craig, you're hurtin' me real bad, sayin' them other homes is better than mine."

We rode to the outskirts of Harrison County in total silence, she smoking furiously, me still sorting out what it meant for Matt that the children she hadn't raised were normal. His behavior had resulted from the brutal, degrading circumstances in which he lived, compounded by the daily interaction with this woman. But we'd found him too late to undo all the damage.

I once agreed with Leora's opinion that only brain damage could account for the massive deficiencies in Matt. Yet his good motor skills, his sporadic bursts of intelligence—writing words, working complicated puzzles—didn't fit that picture clearly.

Matt had been a prisoner all his life, but he still had the will to reach out. I silently promised myself that as soon as Dr. Vogel had completed the evaluation, we'd determine once and for all a plan based on his best interests alone, regardless of his mother.

"Hey, pull over, Miss Craig." Her voice startled me. I stopped the car automatically, wondering if she felt ill. "Look at all that junk." She pointed to the front yard of an old farmhouse, strewn with furniture, books, tables and cartons of pots and pans. TAG SALE, the cardboard sign was lettered, MOVING TOMORROW. EVERYTHING MUST GO.

"Got any beds for sale?" Nellie rolled down her window to yell to the red-faced man, who was clapping his leather mittened hands together. "Follow me," he motioned. She came back a few minutes later, talking to the shivering man.

"Is it okay with you, Miss Craig? He wants t' tie them mattresses onto the roof of your car." She pointed. "I wanna buy a separate bed for Matt. It only costs ten bucks for both them mattresses."

"Sure, Nellie," I had to laugh, "as long as he's got some rope . . ."

"At first ya hurt my feelings on Matt," she said as we drove through town, two mattresses on the roof of the car. "'Bout what ya said t' me, I mean. Cause ya know I've tried t' give him everything. But I think you're right. I also wanted t' keep him a baby. So he's got his own bed now. Counta you said I hadda try t' let him go."

"It's a great start, Nellie. Congratulations." I extended my hand and she slapped hers down so hard my palm burned. We rode together in silence again until we rounded the corner to Burley Street.

"Them other kids—" She began hesitantly. "Them kids looked happy, don't ya think? They got their own lives now. I don't think I should interfere at all. Least not till Matt gets better.

"I was thinkin' though, I dunno, maybe they hadda hurt me real bad on accounta it's the first time I seen them . . . So I'm gonna ask Frankie about it. Maybe in a couple a years me an' him could save enough money t' buy us a house. Then we could ask all my kids if they'd like t' come an' live with us."

A few weeks later, Dr. Vogel's report arrived in a large brown envelope marked confidential:

HARRISON COUNTY BOARD OF EDUCATION

CONFIDENTIAL REPORT
PSYCHIATRIC EVALUATION

Child's Name: Matt Barringer

Address: 319 Burley Street

Referred by: H. C. Counselling Center

Parent or Guardian: Nellie Barringer

This *seven-year-old* boy was carried into my office by his mother, to whom he clung desperately with his arms around her neck and his legs around her waist. (This appears to be a regression from full reports filed by Eleanor Craig, but may have been caused by mutual anxiety.)

He is an attractive youngster, tall for his age. He tests within the normal range on neurological exam. There is nothing stigmatic about his appearance.

Although he was responsive to the tester, he frequently punched and mauled his mother, who gave in to each of his demands. His mother was unable to recall much developmental history and described herself as very upset at the time of his birth, because of the death of her brother.

She spoke of the baby rocking in his crib, a motion which quickly developed into banging his head. She believes he could walk alone at eleven months.

Although there was no evidence of language before this year, apparently this child had the ability to speak much earlier. To date he is able to utter words and phrases clearly, although he does not use complete sentences.

Matt is not toilet trained at home. He does have the sphincteric mechanism necessary to achieve control. He urinates in a corner of the living room floor, occasionally having a bowel movement in the process.

Personal-Social Development: Matt is unable to relate to children or adults in a consistent, meaningful way. He was able to recognize and identify himself in a mirror, and indicated recognition of some of his body parts on request from the examiner. He is able to dress and feed himself but his mother treats him like an infant in both these areas by offering too much assistance. His lack of toilet training and few social successes indicate a marked deviation in this area of development. His personal-social level is in the two- to three-year-old range.

Adaptive Development: Matt's communication problem seems to have caused his failures in this area. He showed a wide range of ability, from the two-and-one-half-year level to what would fall within the norm for his age. He was able to count objects and name colors. He scored age-appropriately in block design and on the sequin form board. The most striking evidence he presented of his retentive memory was not part of the formal test sitution. He spotted a blackboard shaped very much like a TV screen. He then wrote the names of several popular daytime shows which his mother acknowledged watching.

He did not pronounce the words he'd written, even on request, but his spelling was accurate and the letters reproduced without reversals.

Language Development: This is Matt's weakest area. He has only begun to speak within the past year and evidences only a limited vocabulary, although his speech is clear. He is able to imitate two- or three-word phrases, but does not do this with consistency. He uses language only for primitive communication, and not for socialization or to describe inner feelings.

Gross Motor Development: There is no weakness on either side of Matt's body, yet he clearly prefers to be carried by his mother, who in turn appears to encourage this. Nevertheless, balance and tone are good. He coordinates his extremities well.

Fine Motor Development: Matt is right-handed. He strings small beads without difficulty, uses scissors skillfully and is able to cut along a given line. He was able to copy symbols of the circle, triangle and square. His grasping patterns show normal development. His visual-motor skills are entirely normal for a boy his age.

Diagnostic Impression: This has been a difficult child to diagnose. My interest is not really in labeling this boy but in discerning what he is manifesting.

It is impossible to predict how much further he might go cognitively, considering his developmental deviation.

Brain damage is now ruled out. There is no sign of organic-neurologic syndrome. My impression is of a child with many features of atypical ego development.

I would describe his retardation as pseudo-feeblemindedness, the result of maternal and environmental deprivation.

The predominant problem here is this mother's intense need for this child. I was unable to determine why this should be so excessive.

I would hope that eventually the boy will give up his pathological behavior. However, one must consider how this boy views himself. A child allowed to defecate on the floor must think of himself as an animal.

Recommendations: At issue is whether to leave the boy in the home environment. While I understand the possibility of residential placement was rejected earlier, it cannot be ignored at this time in light of this evaluation.

At issue is whether the primary caretaker, his mother, is capable of change.

In a follow-up conference with both parents, I stated that if this boy cannot be toilet trained at home and trained to feed and dress himself independently in a period not to exceed six months, I would firmly recommend that he be removed from the home.

His mother's reaction verged on hysteria, at which point her husband confirmed that four other children were taken from her by the state.

We discussed this and she made a commitment to work more intensively than she has in the past, by her own admission, to train her son in these areas. She will have the support of her therapist, Mrs. Craig.

I suggested that the father have more interaction with the boy, and that he, too, should participate in the child's training.

I hope the next six months will justify postponing consideration of removing Matt from his home.

—*Irwin Vogel, M.D.*

Chapter 16

A glance at my old appointment book confirmed what I'd suspected. It was almost a year since I'd last seen Nellie. A year of many changes for my family. After months of weighing the pros and cons we'd made a major move, several hundred miles north of Harrison County, to an old Victorian farmhouse with a studio where Bill could write.

I found interesting work in a crisis intervention program at a hospital about a half-hour drive from our home. Ellen began commuting by bus to the regional high school. Ann, back from her travels in Africa, was finishing her last semester of college. Richard was living with Billy in Boston and practice teaching at a difficult inner-city school. They all got home less frequently now. I found myself missing them, and Ceil Black, and friends and neighbors we'd left behind.

Ceil kept in touch by phone, often urging me to come for a visit.

"I give up," she'd finally said. "If I'm not enough of an attraction, at least come check up on Nellie and Matt. I'll guarantee it's worth the trip."

I couldn't resist. "Could you make arrangements for me to visit the school next Monday? Then I'll meet you at your office by four o'clock."

I was only vaguely aware of the rolling countryside on the four-hour drive. I found myself reliving each of my contacts with Matt and his family, from Mr. Barringer's first frantic call to the counselling center almost three years ago. I remembered Dr. Diamond's startled assessment: "a kind of case I've read about but never expected to see—a feral child—as wild as if he'd been raised by animals." Then had come my gradual recognition of the intricate and crippling web of defenses with which Nellie had bound herself and her child.

Before we moved Dr. Vogel wrote an enthusiastic re-evaluation of Matt, attributing his most recent development to "the amazing gains his mother had made."

Nellie and I had celebrated with lunch at Howard Johnson's—"This place ain't so stuck up after all."

At first she changed the subject when I talked about my plans to move upstate. "Remember when I couldn't be firm with my son?" she inter-rupted. "Remember I usta try t'keep him a baby? Well, I ain't slept with him once since the day we bought that bed!"

Gradually she came to acknowledge my leav-ing. "Frankie says when you're gone I oughta spend a couple a hours a day walkin' through them downtown stores. He says go have breakfast down the five-an'-ten. But I don't think I have no heart t' keep that up alone."

The last time I saw her she'd announced her own resourceful solution. "Goodbye, Miss Craig." She'd held out her hand. "I guess I won't need ya so much like I thought. I called up that principal where Matt goes t' school. I ast him could I come t' work for them over there. Ya know, cleanin' up them rooms or somethin'. He says I can't be with my son, so if that's what I got in my mind forget it. But it ain't, Miss Craig. It ain't that at all. It's time I did something for somebody else. I don't want no money or nothin' . . ."

So Nellie as well as Matt should be at the school today.

I parked the car as near as I could to the building, and found myself rushing up the flagstone walk.

First I had to see the principal, who wanted to discuss the progress Matt had made.

"We had him in the behavior modification program for awhile," he said. "But Matt had a need to be punished and set himself up to be put in the

'time out' chair. He was being isolated longer and
more frequently, without the results we wanted to
effect. In fact, Matt seemed to like it better when
the teacher had to tie him in.

"His new teacher, Mr. Haggerty, gets further with Matt just by being firm and rewarding
him with praise."

"I can't wait to see him," I finally inter-
jected.

"His class is just returning from a nature
walk. Why not look in on his mother first? She's
helping us out in the library this week. Come on.
I'll walk you down."

Nellie was standing on a high stool, dusting
bookshelves. She looked like a schoolgirl herself, in
a blue denim jumper with a red and white checked
blouse. Her hair had been cut short and curled
softly around her cheekbones. Her face was glowing with natural color.

"Craigie!" She jumped off the high stool and
greeted me with a hug.

"Craigie!" She grinned. "I knew you was
comin', but I didn't know what time. C'mon sit
down." She pulled out a chair at the long library
table. "We're s'posed t' whisper in here but you an'
me can talk 'cause there ain't no classes here now."

We sat beside each other, her hand on my
arm.

"I really like helpin' out at this school." Her
eyes were sparkling. "An' I'm even helpin' with
one a the kids. A girl, fifteen years old. I seen her
come in here with her class—and that girl was actin'

real tough, just the way I usta. So I says t' her teacher, 'I'd like t' talk t' that girl,' 'cause I thought I might be able t' get through t' her.

"An' now she gets fifteen minutes t' talk t' me everyday. An guess what, Miss Craig? That kid is teachin' me how t' read! Whole books, I mean. So we both been helpin' each other, really.

"I like all the teachers now, too. I usta think they acted like the kids was too hard t' handle. But now they treat them like they really love them. They really changed, I mean."

She looked at me and began to laugh. "Oh, I know, Craigie." She slapped my shoulder. "It's me an' Matt that's really changed. Remember when I usta be so shy? Remember I wouldn't never come to a place like this? Well, I had a hard life ya know, but Frankie even says I'm different now.

"An' guess what, Miss Craig? He started a Christmas Club at the bank, so we can get presents for all my other kids.

"An' remember 'bout Matt, how he wouldn't talk at all for all them years? Well awhile ago he started sayin': 'Matt, don't spit,' or 'Matt, sit down,' you know, like teachers say in school. An' now sometimes he even tells me what he wants. God, Miss Craig." Her eyes became misty. "It's such a blessin' t' hear the way that kid can talk.

"An' remember when I was too overprotective? Remember how I wouldn't let him go? Ya won't believe that kid when ya see him now.

"Know what I was thinkin'?" Nellie looked out the window, reflectively. "Know what I wish you'd do? I wish you'd write a whole book bout how me an' Matt has changed. Maybe it would help some other people t' know. Then know what I want ya t' do? When ya gimme the book, I want ya t' put your name in it. How d' ya say it?—autograph it, I mean. Only put 'to Nellie,' not 'to Mrs. Barringer.' An' sign it 'Eleanor,' not 'Miss Craig.' An' I'm gonna keep it always."

Nellie looked up at the clock.

"Ya wanta see my son now?" She got up. "I'll show ya where he is. He oughta be havin' his speech class now."

Nellie pointed to a door across the hall. I tiptoed into the back of the small, bare room. There were no desks—no tables or chairs. Matt and a young woman were sitting cross-legged on a scatter rug with a shoebox full of picture cards between them. Matt's back was to me. His hair looked darker, more brown than I remembered, and cropped closer to his head. He was wearing a light blue, long-sleeved shirt with brown corduroy pants.

"What's the girl doing, Matt?" The teacher held up a picture she'd taken from the box.

He didn't answer until she repeated the question. "What's the girl doing, Matt?"

He took the picture from her hand. "Jumping—rope," he said softly.

"Yes she's jumping rope, but I want you to tell the whole story."

Matt held the card closer, studying it carefully before he spoke.

"The—girl—" he began hesitantly. "The—girl—is—jumping—rope."

Oh, Matt! You're talking in sentences! I wanted to clap and cheer.

The teacher looked up and winked.

"Now what about this boy?"

Matt bent over the second card. "The—boy—" He hesitated again. "The—boy—is—riding his—bike."

"Nice lesson, Matt! I'm sending a good-news note to your teacher." She penciled a message on a lined yellow pad.

"Lollipop?" Matt began to rock.

"No. Not yet. After you read the note." She handed him the paper she'd written on.

"Good news." His voice was high pitched, a hollow monotone. "Good news," he repeated. "Matt had a very good lesson today . . . Lollipop?" he asked again.

"Sure." She tousled his hair affectionately. "Sure you get a lollipop." She pulled four or five from the bottom of the box of pictures. "What color would you like?"

"Green. Green, please." He took it from her hand.

"Okay," she smiled. "But Matt, before you go back to your class, there's someone in our room who'd like to say hello."

"Eeeee," began his familiar, frightened, high-pitched whine. "Eeee—eeee!" He spread his hands over his eyes.

"No, Matt, don't be afraid. It's a friend. Go ahead. Turn around and see."

He turned his body slowly. Spreading his fingers a fraction of an inch he peeked at me, then quickly covered both eyes again.

The whining diminished. He took a second peek, and then a third.

"Hi, Matt!" I smiled.

Still sitting cross-legged, his hands over his eyes, he began to whisper to himself. The volume intensified until I could hear the words. "One?" Then even louder and more excitedly, "Two? Three? One? Two? Three?" He spread his fingers wide enough to view me clearly. "ONE—TWO—THREE!" he cried.

"Yes, Matt," I nodded. "Yes, Matt, it's me."

"Craig! Craig!" He jumped up and came running, his arms outstretched.

"Oh, Matt!" I caught him. "Matt! It's wonderful to see you. I can't believe how much you've learned!" We hugged each other in silence. I felt his hands patting my back.

"Hey, let me look at you. You've grown about four inches, Matt. Your head comes up to my shoulder now. And look at your face. It looks like you must be playing outdoors. You've got freckles all over your nose."

He smiled and touched his nose and then mine. "Craig got freckles, too," he said, "like me."

We both laughed.

"Oh-oh," he looked up at the clock on the

wall. "Eleven o'clock. I hafta go now." His eyes began to dart around, avoiding mine. "I hafta go now!"

"Matt's usually back in his class by eleven," his teacher explained. "Matt, Mrs. Craig can go with you to your room."

Grabbing my wrist he pulled me down the hall. "Oh—oh. Eleven o'clock," he chanted as we ran. "Oh-oh, oh-oh."

I enjoyed being led by Matt, thinking how often I'd seen him carried like an infant to satisfy his mother's needs. I wondered now how far he could go, how much he could narrow that gap between himself and children whose early days had provided both nurture and growth.

Perhaps he'd never relate with easy social grace. But he was progressing. For now that had to be enough. Suddenly he stopped and stared into an open classroom.

"Oh here you are, Matt." His teacher looked up from the book he was reading to a group of boys. "And you've brought us a visitor." He smiled at me. "Why don't you both come in?"

But Matt lingered in the hallway, looking at me searchingly. He let go of my wrist and began to stroke my arm.

"Bye now, Craig," he whispered, and nuzzled his head against my shoulder. I felt a surge of compassion for Nellie. How hard it was to let him go. Yet he and I both knew the time had come.

He took a few steps toward the room, then

looked back and smiled. "Bye now, Craig." He waved with a flicker of his hand. "Bye now."

Matt, I wanted to say, Matt, I'll remember you always. But he had already walked into his class alone.

I hurried down the hall and pushed my shoulder against the heavy wooden door. The sunlight hit my face and suddenly it was impossible to hold back the tears.

With blurred vision I put my hand on the metal railing and began to grope for a footing on the concrete stairs. Suddenly, as clearly as if it were happening again, I had a mental image of Matt on the stairs at the clinic the day he'd begun to count. "Wun, doo, dree." His voice resounded in my mind.

I stopped on the bottom step to wipe my cheeks, feeling foolish now to be both teary-eyed and grinning, too.

Bye now, Matt. I looked back up at the school. Bye now. Bye now.